TEX-MAR SEMINARS AND PUBLICATIONS would like to express our thanks to those many individuals and corporations contributing to the development of this seminar and publication: Butterick Marketing (Vogue/Butterick Patterns); Pfaff Sewing Machine Company; Burda Patterns; Doreen Miller: Laurie Thomas; Hendy Cameron, Knit and Stretch Sewing; Larry Soloman; N. Jefferson; Cantex, Wescan Agencies — Bernina Sewing Machines; Sue Ferguson; Marge Brown; Palmer Pletsch Associates who have shared with us all their groundwork with Overlock Sergers in their book "Sewing With Sergers" and relating seminars.

COVER GRAPHICS & DESIGN:	KARIN JAGER, VALERIE YATES
ILLUSTRATION & GRAPHICS:	ANN WONG, MARC BAUR, R.D. HOOEY
TYPESETTING:	TICK SET – TERRY & IRENE CHARLES
PRINTED BY:	METROPOLITAN PRESS
PUBLISHED BY:	TEX-MAR SEMINARS AND PUBLICATIONS No. 57 - 10220 Dunoon Dr. Richmond, B. C. V7A 1V6

PRINTED IN CANADA 1986

ISBN -0- 920207-01-4

First Printing January 1984

Second Printing August 1986

Hazel Boyd Hooey

HAZEL BOYD HOOEY is a nationally known and respected textile authority, instructor and author. COUTURE ACTION KNITS and SILKS 'N SATINS were her first two successful publications. This is Ms Boyd Hooey's second printing of Couture Action Knits, now updated and revised.

In the development of her seminars and this book, she has again drawn on her vast textile and sewing experience to up-date and re-vamp an important portion the sewing family; THE KNIT.

Formerly, Canadian Director for "Knit and Stretch" Sewing, she was responsible for development of the Canadian market and recruitment and teacher training across Canada. Further, drawing from her pattern and dress design experience (3 years study in haute couture and pattern drafting under European instruction), seamstress, instructor (Bishop Method and Knit and Stretch) along with a 6 year retail fabric store partnership, she brings a wealth of ideas with time and labour saving techniques.

Presently, in addition to her involvement in seminar development for TEX-MAR SEMINARS, she is active as an independent sales representative (past 12 years) for several eastern fabric, lace and notion suppliers.

In spite of her hectic schedule, she does spend some time at the mountain chalet with family and friends. This is where she does most of her design, sewing and wardrobe creation. Proverbs 31: 10 through 20 accurately profiles this active lady.

TABLE OF CONTENTS

Forward

With the 60's came the great interest in knit and stretch sewing. Hendy Cameron published the first (original) book detailing the subject, and homesewers embarked on sewing polyester double knits, T-shirts, bathing suits and even sweaters.

As with history, this period of excitement waned as these new fabrics became "common-place" and fashion designers tired of working with the "new" synthetic knits. Many women today, still imagine the old "polyester double knit" when knits are mentioned.

This updated and revised edition of **Couture Action Knits** attempts to expand your horizons, seeking out the newest, exciting knits again catching the interest and the excitement of designers and home sewers alike. We are featuring many of the finest designs and fabrics now entering the marketplace; silk knits, ultra matte jersey, patterned sweater knits, and the latest "action wear" fabrics.

You can quickly create comfortable, carefree and yet professionally styled clothing with our easy time-saving methods using the revolutionary, new **Overlock Sergers**, now available to home sewers.

This book is not intended to replace your basic sewing book but is designed to focus on specialized techniques in working with knit or stretch fabrics.

SUCCESSFUL SEWING!

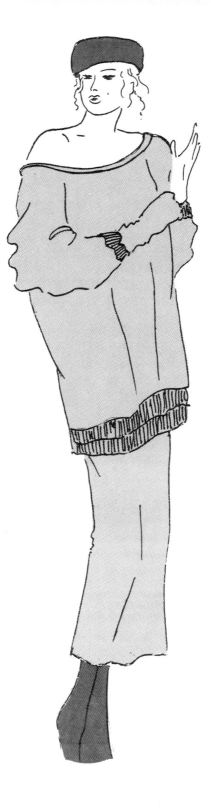

Types of Stretch Fabrics

VERTICAL STRETCH —Usually used in ski, stirrup or stretch corduroy pants.

HORIZONTAL STRETCH—Stretch circles around the body for comfort. Most common stretch used in T-shirts, dresses, slacks, jackets, etc. Garments will be uncomfortable unless stretch is used correctly.

TWO-WAY STRETCH —Used in "**Action**" garments; body-suits, dance-wear, skating and in many new ultra-matte jerseys. Used in body-hugging and drapable garments. Generally one direction stretches more than the other and this should go around the body.

KNIT FABRIC IDENTIFICATION

- *Single Knit* — Plain knit fabric with a smooth finish on right side. Has a definite right and wrong side. It is also called jersey. It is usually soft and drapable.

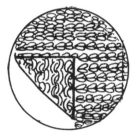

- *Double Knit* — Two sets of stitches locked together in knitting process producing a fabric that looks finished on both sides. Usually have a much firmer hand and therefore can be inter-changed with wovens in pattern styles.

- *Rib Knit* — Has pronounced vertical ridges. Usually very stretchy on the crossgrain. Can be one plain and one perle or two plain and two perle as in knitting terms. Poly/cotton or nylon are the most common yarns used, each giving different amounts of stretch. Can be used for neck, sleeve, hem edges and complete body-hugging garments.

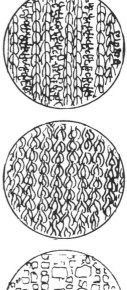

- *Interlock Knits* — Made by interlocking stitches. It is similar to double knit in appearance as both sides look finished. However, this fabric can develop runs at one of the crosswise edges. Determine which edge by stretching on the crosswise grain. Then place hem and other crosswise seams in the direction of the non-running edge.

- *Raschel Knit* — Has limited stretch on the crosswise grain and none on the vertical. On the back side you will see rows of straight threads which stabilize as they are knitted into fabric. It could be mistaken for a woven fabric. Interesting textures can be produced with this method.

- *Tricot Knits*— Soft drapable single knit which has a smooth face depicting the right side and a definite wrong side. If in doubt, pull fabric crossgrain and it will always roll to the right side. This type of knit is quite often in jersey type prints, as well as lingerie fabrics. It only stretches on the crossgrain.

Each Knit or Stretch type fabric comes in several different qualities. Some are pure fibres, others are blends. Each quality has it's own peculiarities concerning shrinkage and care.

On the following pages we give a detailed listing of the most common types of stretch fabrics.

Types of Stretch Fabrics

TYPE	CONTENT	QUALITIES	CARE	SHRINKAGE	APPLICATION
INTERLOCK	100% Cotton Interlock	soft; sometimes stripes or prints	Machine wash Dryer: med.-hot	up to 5"/m	- Sportswear - Tops
INTERLOCK	50/50 Poly/cotton	soft but with body; good crosswise stretch	same as above	up to 2½"/m	- Sportwear - Dresses,tops
INTERLOCK JERSEY	100% Polyester	same as above: quick drying if transfer printer; wrong side has whitish color; quite luxurious finish	Machine wash: Permanent Press cycle Dryer: cool	minimal up to 1"/meter	- Dresses - Tops - drapery style
INTERLOCK	Spun Polyester	very soft and drapey; will pill in most cases	same as above	up to 2"/m	- Dresses - Tops, fluid styles
SINGLE KNIT	50/50 Poly/cotton	soft, plains, stripes, prints; definite right and wrong side; edges will sometimes stretch; moderate crosswise stretch	Machine wash: medium-hot	up to 2-3" per meter	- Fuller styles - T-shirt styles
DOUBLE KNIT	100% Polyester	wrinkleproof; stable to sew; rather heavy and rigid; doesn't breathe unless treated with a Zelcon finish	Machine wash: Permanent press cycle Dryer: cool	up to 2"/m	- Suits - Jackets - Slacks
DOUBLE KNIT	50/50 Poly/cotton	very soft; stable to sew; 2 face construction; stitches the same on both sides; breathes	same as above	up to 2½"/m	- Tennis Dresses - Sportswear - Shorts - Dresses
DOUBLE KNIT	Orlon/Acrylic	very soft; most wool like synthetic; sometimes pills; usually plain	same as above	up to 2½"/m	- Lightweight suits - Jackets - Dresses and tops
DOUBLE KNIT	Wool	gives tailored-classic look; holds crease well for slacks; firm for sewing	Dryclean **Preshrink at drycleaners**	up to 2½'/m	- Jackets, suits - Dresses - Topstitching ideal

Fabric	Content	Characteristics	Care	Stretch	Uses
FLEECE BACK KNIT	50/50 Poly/cotton	cozy, warm texture; fleece absorbs perpiration; comfortable for wearing	Machine wash Dryer: Medium	up to 3"/m	- Jogging suits - Jump suits - Tops, jackets and general sportswear
JERSEY	Check contents on above types and treat accordingly	soft and clingy, stretchable; flat, smooth, single knit; luxurious in wool; sporty in cotton; supple and drapey in rayon, silk or polyester			- Loosely fitted flowing styles, gathers or draped styles
WARP KNIT	Various blends	tricot and raschel knit most common fabrics; runproof and limited stretchability usually cross grain only			
SWEATER KNITS	Same as jersey	springy and resilient; sometimes much like handknitting	Dryclean or Cool handwash		- Simple styles - Cardigans, unlined dresses
SILK KNITS	100% Silk	much like handknitted; cool to wear See **SILKS N' SATINS** book	Handwash - squeeze out moisture in towel. Flat dry.	up to 3"/m	- Same as above
STRETCH TERRY STRETCH VELOUR	50/50 Poly/Cotton	plush surface; loops on surface; brilliant solid colors and stripes; very stretchy	Machine wash: Medium Dryer: Medium	up to 3-5" per meter	- Joffing suits - Sportswear, tops - Loungewear
TWO-WAY STRETCH	Cotton/polyester/ Spandex	very strong and durable; breathes; smooth fiber; lightweight; stripes, dots, plains	Machine wash/dry cool perm press Drip Dry also	up to 1-2" per meter	- Casual sportswear - Dancewear, leotards - Separates, dresses
TWO WAY STRETCH	Spandex/polyester or Nylon	very strong and durable; extremely comfortable; will hold body heat; plain colors and swim prints	same as above	minimal	- Swimwear - Actionwear garments - Body hugging styles dresses, tops
TRICOT	100% Nylon, acetate, etc.	very lightweight knit; stable lengthwise; very stretchable crosswise; some wet look cire	Machine wash/dry Delicate	very minimal	- Loungewear - Lingerie - Sportswear Lining for knits

Styles to Suit

CHOOSING YOUR PATTERN

On Fabric Chart (see pages 10 & 11) you will notice style suggestions in the last column for each type listed. Consult this **prior** to purchase of your fabric and pattern.

COMMERCIAL PATTERNS

Many patterns list both woven and knit fabrics, as for these styles, the stretch factor is less important than the weight and texture chosen in fabric. For comparison, if the pattern is of a soft, flowing style, a fluid jersey or interlock knit may be as suitable as a woven challis. Stable, single and double knits easily substitute for woven fabrics with many patterns. However, in many cases, only a knit may be suitable. When the stretch factor is important to fit and style in a pattern, there is usually a stretch gauge printed on pattern envelope. Use this stretch gauge as a test for stretch-ability of your fabric. Refer to page 17. We include a common stretch gauge for reference (see pages 17 & 18). Many patterns call for use of stretch fabrics, so we include a comparative chart of the various Stretch Terminologies in use by the pattern companies.

WHAT SIZE DO I CHOOSE?

You may use one size smaller on regular patterns suggesting woven fabrics as knits have their own built-in ease. This applies to moderately stretchy knits. Wool double knits of heavier weights may be used with regular sizing (especially for suitings) where more ease is required. Many patterns have multiple sizing, which is ideal for knits as easy adjustments can be attained. Follow your pattern instructions in using graded lines for your figure type and fitting problems.

If using **ribbed** or excessively stretchy fabrics where a body-hugging style is chosen consult Page 50, Ribbing.

HOW MUCH EASE DO I NEED?

For wearing comfort, most commercial patterns allow 2 inches (5cm) of ease or excess fabric over your body measurements for dresses, slacks, skirts, etc., and 4 inches (10cm) for jackets. Due to built-in give and comfort factor with knits, unless design warrants, this much ease is not required. Generally 1 inch (2.5cm) is ample ease around hip area, for fitted styles. Flat measure your pattern against your measurements and double check, before cutting your fabric and pattern. Adjust accordingly and keep in mind you are usually measuring one-half of pattern, so be sure to double your measurements.

SUITABLE FABRICS

Keep current issues of pattern magazines handy as often they feature actual photographs of garments made up in their patterns. This helps you visualize many of the suitable knits for those fashion styles. Window shop in ready-to-wear stores too! Frequently, patterns are available for similar garment styles that interest you or ones you'd like to create. Notice that most knits look better with less seam detail. However, they lend themselves to top-stitching giving a smart tailored look.

> KNIT TIP: *When laying out patterns, keep in mind, the possibility of using scraps for a child's garment. Yokes, sleeves, etc., can be attractive in contrasting colors so it is not always necessary to have a complete garment sized piece. Remember, however, do not go "off-grain" or your garment will twist.*

DRAPE THE FABRIC

When you find a fabric you like, drape it over yourself and view in a mirror. This will give you a better feeling for the fabric, it's character and assist in visualizing it made up in your chosen style. **Don't forget to rewind and replace on the shelf!**

FULL LENGTH MIRROR *is a must for the serious seamstress. Check at each stage of garment construction for the detail development as well as a total head-to-toe general appearance.*

Terminology for Stretch Gauges

Amount of Stretch	McCall's	Vogue	Butterick	Simplicity	Kwik-Sew
18%	–	–	–	18%	18%
25%	–	–	–	20%	25%
35%	Stretch Knit	Moderate Stretch	Moderate Stretch	35%	35%
50%	1-way stretch 2-way stretch	2-way stretch	2-way stretch	50%	50%
70%	–	–	–	70%	70%

SELECTION OF CORRECT KNIT is important to garment fit. Test the knit choice against the stretch gauge (printed on pattern envelope) as most grading systems differ from individual pattern companies. We've included a stretch gauge for reference. For two-way stretch, test against a gauge for both crosswise and lengthwise direction. To use a stretch gauge, fold over the edge of knit fabric about 3 inches (7.5cm). Place the 4 inch (10cm) strip of folded knit against gauges and stretch **gently** from line to outer edge. If fabric stretches without excessive rolling to outer line or even farther, your fabric has the necessary amount of stretch for the pattern. For more information on selection of suitable knit fabrics, see pages 10 & 11.

Stretch Gauges

Fabric with 18% stretch across the grain such as single and double knits.

4" (10cm) of Knit fabric should stretch to at least here.

Fabric with 25% stretch across the grain such as nylon tricot, velour, interlock.

4" (10cm) of Knit fabric should stretch to at least here.

Fabric with 35% stretch across the grain such as sweater knit, velour, terry, interlock of fabric with Spandex or Lycra contents.

4" (10cm) of Knit fabric should stretch to at least here.

Fabric with 50% stretch such as swimsuit fabric, fabric with Spandex or Lycra content.

4" (10cm) of knit fabric should stretch to at least here.

Fabric with 70% stretch such as swimsuit fabric, power net, girdle fabrics.

4" (10cm) of knit fabric should stretch to at least here.

Fabric with 100% stretch across grain such as ribbing.

4" (10cm) of knit fabric should stretch to at least here.

Fabric Preparation

Prior to laying out and cutting, **Pre-shrink fabric** in the same manner planned for the finished garment. If it will be machine washed and dryed, then follow that method. If it is to be drycleaned, (most wools are best this method) take fabric to dry-cleaners and have it steamed or

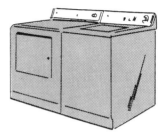

pre-shrunk. If you wish to steam at home, lay fabric on a bed holding iron closely over top (2 inches (5cm) above) while moving iron slowly over entire piece of fabric. You may use an old sheet to protect bed.

Many cotton and cotton blend knits lose surface finish during pre-shrinking. To renew finish you may use a fabric finish spray (not a starch). This will assist in keeping seams flat and easier to stitch (if seams tend to roll after cutting). Approximate shrinkages are listed on Fabric Chart, pages 10 &11. Allow for this when purchasing fabric.

Notions and Accessories

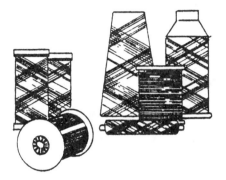

THREAD

All polyester and polyester/cotton threads are strong and elastic, making them especially suited for knits. They have many other features; shrink and tear resistant, soft-fine, washfast, fade resistant. Nylon thread is very strong and best used on nylon knits. One of the newest threads available for the homesewer is a "fuzzy" looking thread called either **"Woolley Lock"**™ **Nylon** or **Stretchy Nylon**. The majority of major thread companies will probably have a comparable product available very soon. It has a yarn-like texture that creates a very soft but strong edge or seam. It can be used on the loopers and/or needle(s) of a serger. Because of the soft finish, it produces an attractive rolled edge. One **caution** however, if you are planning on ironing your garment later you will require a cool setting! If used in the bobbin on a regular sewing machine (very difficult to thread through the needle without a threader) in combination with a twin needle on top, a very professional looking finish can be achieved on the neck edges and hem areas of bodysuits and regular knit fashions. The tremendous stretch achieved is excellent for knits. See page 115, Bodysuits. However, if not available, the use of polyester thread is acceptable, as it also has stretch.

Two-way stretch knits and bathing suit fabrics require a strong synthetic thread. The polyester spun, long fibre threads available at this writing are generally suitable for all types of knits, even natural fibres. The cotton wrapped polyester would be suitable especially for wool double or single knits. With the cotton next to the wool fabric it would diminish the possibility of the thread cutting the seam because of it's strength.

SERGER THREAD —
see page 56 Overlock Serging Machines.

TOPSTITCHING THREAD

Buttonhole twist thread is available in several varieties for use as topstitiching. Use a longer stitch and a size 14 or 16 needle, stitching **slowly**. Use a contrast shade for an interesting effect on top thread and your regular colour in bobbin. If you have difficulty sewing a straight stitching line, place a piece of "magic tape" on garment and stitch along it's edge. You may also use a "quilter-guide bar" which rests on the outside edge or line to be followed. **Can't find the right colour?** Combine two thicknesses of your regular thread and thread onto machine as one, lengthening your stitch.

ZIPPERS

Lightweight flexible zippers are available so choose one suitable for the fabric selected. Nylon or polyester zippers with knitted tapes are best. Zippers are rarely necessary unless you have a high tight neck and a fairly firm knit fabric.

PINS AND NEEDLES

Use the long, glass headed pins or the new ball point pins. Ball point, blue or stretch needles help prevent skipped stitches as the needle **rolls** between fabric yarns rather than piercing them. This is particularly important with polyester fabrics. If you continue to have skipped stitches after trying different needles, you may have a build up of residue from the polyester yarns. Try some rubbing alcohol to clean needle. For wool, silk and cotton knits a regular needle works fine. Needle sizes should be a "9" for fine fabrics and an 11 (65/70) to 14 (80/90) for medium or heavier knits.

BALL POINT NEEDLE

DO NOT SKIMP ON NEEDLES! Use a fresh needle (discard the old one) with each garment unless you are **certain** you did not **HIT** any pins, should you be pinning your garments. Dull needles cause snags and runs in knits. For best results do not treat knits like wovens.

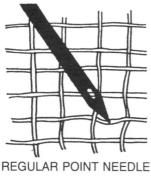

REGULAR POINT NEEDLE

Twin Needles come in different sizes and widths. Topstitching can be very attractive (and straight!) when using a twin needle. See chapter 21 for ideas.

BUTTONS

Simple styling with buttons adds class to a garment. Again, look to your ready to wear garments for inspiration. Covered buttons may not always be the answer as they can project that **"Loving Hands At Home" image at times. Some buttons feature an action motif (sail-boats, tennis, or golf, etc.) and are great as a final touch on sporty knits.**

GRIPPER SNAPS

Many types are available locally; Coloured enamel, Silver, Gold, Old West style, Fabric (see through) metal snaps, Snaps attached to twill tape.

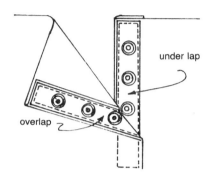

under lap

overlap

Application — If using individual snaps on sport knits, ⅝"(1.5cm) to ¾" (1.7cm) grosgrain (polyester only) sewn on your garment prior to application gives a firm finish, eliminating the need for interfacing. Most basic colours are now available in grosgrain so matching or co-ordination would not be a problem. Most gripper snap packages have some detailed instruction techniques, so check before applying snaps.

MARKING EQUIPMENT

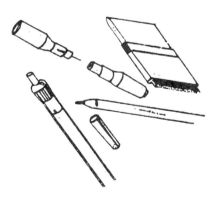

Tracing wheels do not work well on knits in that they have soft surfaces which tend to cause the wheel to cut through the paper. Dressmaker's pencils come in different colours and the new water soluble or evaporating marking pens are excellent. Don't forget that the garment must be sewn within 24 hours or the marks disappear! See Layout and Cutting, page 43.

Tape a small paper sack on the edge of your sewing table. A perfect catch-all for your snipped threads and seam or trim cuttings.

22

SHEER TRICOT BIAS SEAMS FINISH

Narrow ⅝" (1.5cm) sheer seam binding is available by the package for finishing the seam edges on loosely woven knits (bulky types) in areas where there will be exposure. Although it is not necessary to prevent fraying, it will give a "couturier" finish on unlined jackets where you have pressed open seams, especially if you do not have a serger for finishing. This sheer tricot binding comes in white, black, and beige. It is very easy to apply as it rolls over the edge as you gently pull it. I find a multiple zig-zag stitch works best.

SCISSORS AND SHEARS

Synthetic fabrics tend to dull your scissors. It is amazingly inexpensive to have your shears sharpened. There are special Polyester shears which have a serrated edge (not pinking shears) which are excellent for knits in general. Invest in a good pair of scissors and then hide them, **for your use only!**

ROTARY CUTTERS

Watch your fingers — they are very sharp! These cutting tools are extremely quick and accurate to use. Use weights to hold the pattern onto fabric. These can be purchased or use what you have, glass furniture castors, ashtrays, etc. A special **cutting mat must be used** to protect blade and table surface. The largest size possible is advisable, otherwise you are constantly moving the mat in order 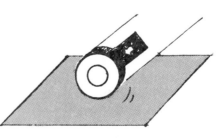 to continue cutting. They do have sizes up to 48" x 96" (122 x 244cm) which have one inch (2.5cm) squares for easy alignment. These mats roll for easy storage and will be a lifetime investment. It may be necessary to special order the larger mats as they are not often carried in the stores. The cutters are available with or without a seam guide.

The guide can be removed if needed. The guide works well with patterns that do not have seam allowances included. Several thicknesses can be cut at one time if you are cutting more than one garment. Once you have mastered it, this method for cutting is much quicker. See page 43, Layout and Cutting.

PRE-FINISHED COLLARS AND CUFFS

These are available in a variety of colours (some with pin stripes and full stripes) and lend a professional touch to your sportswear and dresses. They are not available in all stores but keep a lookout and you may find them.

APPLIQUES

Children's sports motifs, iron-on initials, all add a personal and special touch. Apply in a similar fashion to fusible interfacing techniques. See page 121 for suggestions.

ELASTICS

Non-roll is best for waistbands, softer stretch for lingerie, loungewear and chlorine treated for swimwear and bodysuits (retains elasticity even when wet). If elastic is enclosed, a chlorine treated type will stand up extremely well with washing and dry-cleaning.

Transparent Elastic is a revolutionary new polyurathane elastic on the market which comes in three widths, ¼" (6mm), ⅜"(10mm), and ½" (12mm). It is clear in appearance, has excellent memory, chlorine treated, and is very thin (there are several weights or qualities available). It is used in exclusive imported lingerie and aerobic wear. It would give much less bulk to the edges of these garments. Serger sewing on this weight of elastic would give a more uniform stitch. See page 97, Elastic Applications.

PIPING

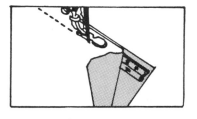

PIPING SEWN

Many decorative pipings are available to enhance seams; satin, polyester and poly/cotton. Apply it on edge seams, dropped shoulder seams, raglan, and even centre seams for design effect. **Preshrink pipings** prior to applying as they most often use a cotton string inside.

Detailing with fold-over braids and striped trims for sportswear garments add a decorative touch. Twill tape (pre-shrink if cotton) can also be used for detail as well as applying it to shoulder seams and areas where you need stabilization.

FRAY CHECK/FRAY NO MORE

This clear plastic liquid can be used to keep buttonholes, corners and pockets, etc. from fraying out. The liquid will dry darker so apply very cautiously. Use a toothpick to apply in tiny areas. It will handle laundering and drycleaning. This is a quick way to stabilize the thread ends from **serger seams.**

OVERLOCK SERGING NOTIONS —
See Page 67, Overlock Serger Machines.

Handy grab all storage unit may be made from a mug rack hung on the wall. Use for notion and tools needed often.

Shoulder Pads

Use shoulder pads to fill out and give support to areas where definition is required. Knit dresses and jackets seem to have a more finished look if the shoulders are defined. Fashion however, seems to dictate when it is applicable to use them. These may be purchased or self-made in a variety of shapes and sizes. We've included the main ones used in women's wear.

Cover shoulder pads with lightweight silky fabric. This gives an attractive finish for an unlined garment. It also eliminates obvious show through to the right side of garment, if using a light fabric. Nylon tricot fabric in a matching colour also works well. Cut your fabric on the bias for ease in shaping over the pad allowing 1″ (2.5cm) seams. On underside, tack lining to pad by folding back, working across pad with slanted basting stitches. Catch tiny stitches on lining side. Place top piece on, pin in place and serge stitch edges together.

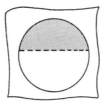

1. ¼″ (6mm); ½″ (1.3cm) used for set-in sleeves in dresses, blouses, jackets. These are normally pre-covered in an acetate lining with finished or unfinished edges.

2. 1″ (2.5cm) used for set-in sleeves in lined coats and jackets. This pad extends below the shoulder providing a smooth foundation in the upper chest area, a common problem for most women.

3. ¼″ (6mm); ½″ (1.3cm); 1″ (2.5cm) used for raglan, dolman or kimono sleeves and dropped shoulders. Use ¼″ (6mm) for blouses, sweaters and for lightweight dresses and ½″ (1.3cm) for dresses and soft jackets. Use 1″ (2.5cm) for lined coats and

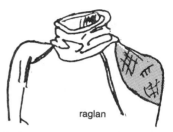

raglan

jackets. Often the sleeve portion of the pad is broader than shown which gives an extended shoulder look.

EASY APPLICATION

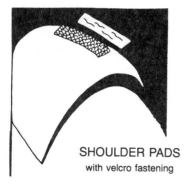

SHOULDER PADS
with velcro fastening

Try using Velcro or Fix Velour for applying shoulder pads to garment. The pads can then be easily removed for washing and drycleaning, not to mention the ease in packing for travel and pressing the garment. The smaller button type may also be used.

See "Shoulder Pad Camisole" Page 127.

Interfacing for Knits

Choosing the correct interfacing for your knit garment can enhance or ruin the overall look. You will find a complete, comparative interfacing chart covering the majority of brands available locally, on pages 30 & 31. When you are selecting interfacing for knits, consideration should be given to the stretch and recovery properties. A balance must be correct for the desired outcome. We choose the weight in conjunction with the fabric weight. Place fabric and interfacing together then test for durability and show through to the right side. Today, a vast assortment of colours are available; nude, white, black, charcoal, and grey. Other colours are available in the U.S. Keep in mind the intent when the selection is made. Purchase several yards (metres) of different types of your choice. Pre-shrink those needing it and they will then be ready for cutting whenever you require them.

WOVEN INTERFACING

Unless cut on the bias, this type does not have any stretch or recovery properties. Suitable areas for this type would be a tab front, cuffs, facing, etc. where no give is needed. There are several new, very lightweight woven fusibles that would be excellent with compatible fine single knits, where minimal shaping is desired.

NON-WOVEN FUSIBLE

This is the most desirable choice. It takes on the characteristics of knits and allows fabric to stretch and recover normally. The majority of non-woven fusibles have crosswise stretch but retain lengthwise stability which prevents stretching in vertical buttonholes, waistbands or pockets, etc. If you choose a non-woven with a crosswise stretch you will need to run the stretch up and down when using **horizontal buttonholes** to prevent gaping.

These do not generally shrink but, prior to cutting you may check by placing a pressing cloth on ironing board, then interfacing with fusible side down. Hold steam iron 2 inches (5cm) above. You may see the interfacing pull in slightly. Continue with steaming until this action stops. A non-woven, non-fusible is not recommended for use with knits.

PRE-TEST INTERFACINGS

Always pre-test combinations of fabric and interfacings. The majority of fusibles tend to give a stiffer hand after fusing. On lightweight knits, white has a tendency to show through, whereas nude or ivory does not detract from the colour. You may also require the use of several interfacing types in one garment to achieve stability, give body and produce your desired effect. It is possible to fuse additional layers on top until you like the firmness.

PRE-SHRINK WOVEN OR KNITTED FUSIBLES

Hand immerse interfacing piece in **hot** water. This does not harm it's fusibility as resin is activated only at higher boiling temperature (300 deg.F). Soak for approximately 20 minutes. Do not rub the fabric as this tends to remove fusible surface finish. Roll in towel to remove all excess moisture and hang over shower rod to dry.

INTERFACING AREAS

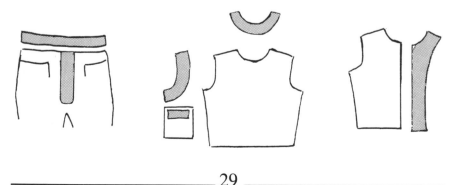

Interfacing for Knits

SUITABLE FUSIBLE INTERFACING FOR KNITS

	FABRIC NAME	TYPE	WEIGHT	FIBRE CONTENT	COLORS	USE
★★	Sylemaker 601	Woven	Light	60% Poly 40% Rayon	W, Bl	- non stretch, fine
⊗	Easy Knit	knit	light	100% nylon	W, Bl, B, G	- soft drapable tricot with crosswise stretch & lengthwise stability
••	Knit Shape		"	"	Bl, B, C	"
★★	Fuse A Knit		"	"	W, Bl, B	"
■	Poly "O"	non-woven	sheer	100% polyester	W, B, C	- no show through - crosswise & lengthwise stretch - stability for sheer - ltwt fabrics
••	Sheer Shape		"	"	W, B	"
★★	Stylease		ltwt	"	W, B, C	"
★★	Stylease Sheer		sheer	"	"	"
••	Shape Well	woven	med wt	100% cotton	W	- woven med wt, cut on bias for knits, adheres well
⊗	Shape Flex	woven	ltwt	"	W, Bl	- woven ltwt - cut on bias for knits
■	All-Purpose		"	"	W, Bl, B	- adheres well
■	Every Purpose		"	"	"	"
★★	Presto		"	"	"	"
★★	Presto Sheer		sheer	"	"	- super for ltwt jersey, silk knits
■	Jiffy Flex	Non-woven	1. super ltwt	100% polyester	W	- crosswise stretch
			2. ltwt	80% poly/20% nylon	W, C	- soft, flexible shaping - single knits & ltwt knits
			3. suitwt	80% poly/20% nylon	W, C	- med weight knits, suits
⊗	Easy Shaper		ltwt	70% nylon/20% poly/10% rayon	W, C	- same as Jiffy Flex #2
			suitwt		W, C	- same as Jiffy Flex #3
★★	Lastick		med wt	100% poly	W	- stretches & recovers

	Name	Construction	Weight	Fiber Content	Colors	Notes
★★	Stylemaker 603	woven brushed	med	56% rayon/44% cotton	W, B	- brushed surface, soft shaping, non-stretchy, suits
●●	Sof-Shape	non-woven	lt to med	100% nylon	W, B, G	- for soft natural shaping - brushed surface, soft shaping - crosswise and bias stretch
■	Shape-up	"	med	100% spunlaced poly	W	- suitings & double knits
●●	Feather Shape	"	"	60% viscose, 40% nylon computer dot	W	" "
⊗	Suit Shape	woven weft insertion	med	84% poly, 16% nylon	G, W	- brushed surface suit wt & heavier knits
★★	Stylemaker 602	"	"	60% poly, 40% rayon	G, W	- cut on bias for knits
■	Suitmaker Fusible	woven	med	48% cotton, 39% rayon, 13% goat's hair	B	- heavier suits, coats
⊗	Sure-fuse	non-woven	lt wt	65% poly, 35% rayon	W, B	- firmer - not as good for knits
★★	Midshape	"	med wt	50% poly, 50% nylon	W	" "
★★	Stylease Medium	"	med wt	100% poly	W	" "
■	Non-woven Fusible	"	med wt	100% rayon	W, B	" non-stretchy

PATTERN TRACING CLOTHS — NOT INTERFACINGS

	Name		Weight		Colors	Notes
⊗	Trace a Pattern		lwt		W, Plain	- for tracing patterns from master. - Altering or designing
⊗	Stacy's Tracer		"	1" sq. grid	W with blue dots	
■	Pattern Tracing Cloth		"		W with red dots	- dots show grain line easily
●●	Stitch & Tear		firm	50% rayon, 50% acetate	W	- rip away backing for decorative work, buttonholes
⊗	Trace Erase		firm	"	W	" "

Fabric Company Codes:
- ⊗ Stacy Fabrics Corp.
- ■ Staple Sewing Aids
- ★★ J. N. Harper
- ●● Pellon Corp.

Colors:
- W - white
- Bl - black
- B - beige
- C - charcoal
- G - grey

PRE-SHRINK FUSIBLE INTERFACINGS
SEE PAGE 29

Necklines, tabs, waistbands, collars, cuffs and facings should all be interfaced. Interfacing helps retain detailing and stability while preventing excess stretching. Patterns do not always suggest interfacing in areas where it would be beneficial. For example a dress with a bias back diagonal seam on the skirt section needs to be stabilized with interfacing on the facing side of the opening. Patch pockets should be interfaced on the top hem, especially with knits, as they tend to stretch out when putting your hands in and out. **Fusing on the facing side** is generally suggested. This eliminates any possibility of showing through. It is not normally necessary to interface hemlines as this often detracts from the softness desired in a knit garment. Obvious drapey styled areas should be excluded. One exception is your jacket hem. Mark hemline with basting stitches, or press up a hem width. Next, serge or machine finish raw edge. Cut a bias piece (if woven type) of fusible interfacing the same length as hem, piecing as necessary. Iron interfacing to wrong side of hem using standard application techniques. Hem garment using a blind catch stitch (see page 110) easing in fullness where necessary and press.

HERE'S HOW TO FUSE

1. Place pattern piece carefully on interfacing so the grainline arrow on pattern follows the lengthwise grain direction of interfacing. The one exception would be a garment front where horizontal buttonholes will be used with a stretchable interfacing. In this case, use the stretch running with grain. This eliminates "fish-mouthed" buttonholes. Cut.

2. Trim away ½ inch (1.3cm) of seam allowances. The remaining ⅛ inch (0.3cm) is stitched into seam in the event of future release of your interfacing at some point. Trim ¼ inch (0.6cm) off corners to reduce bulk.

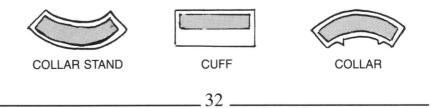

COLLAR STAND   CUFF   COLLAR

3. Place coated side of interfacing on wrong side of fashion fabric facing. Cover with damp press cloth and apply steam and pressure for ten seconds (count slowly) with iron set on "wool". Do not slide iron. Turn fabric over and using a press cloth repeat for an additional ten seconds.

press cloth
interfacing
fabric

PATTERN FOLDER: *Take a letter size file folder and tape the sides together. Paste the front and back of pattern envelope to folder covers. This allows traced patterns to be reused and also packed easily. Use a file box as a reference system for fashions and ideas.*

TAPE

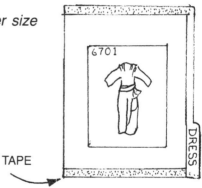

TOP LAYER OF FABRIC FEEDING UNEVENLY?
Try lifting presser foot very slightly while sewing. Don't raise the foot...lighten as you sew. Works great!

Fast Fitting Tips

SHRINKING OUT DART

Fit problems are diminished tre-mendously with knit fabrics. Shou-lder problems, bust fit, etc., are all minimized. You may even be able to delete bust darts completely, dependent upon stretch of your fabric. To eliminate darts and retain ease you can put a basting stitch starting one inch (2.5cm) below dart. Place garment front and back seams together. Pull basting thread up to fit. **Shrink out gathers** over a tailor's ham. Take out fullness and at same time shape your garment. This method is exceptionally good with striped knits.

SWAY BACK

This is not automatically eliminated with knits as it is a flat back situation and not one of fullness. If you regularly delete one inch (2.5cm) at garment center back then continue to do so with a knit dress, slacks or skirt. Any major fitting or figure problem should be corrected in similar manner as for woven fabrics.

WAIST EASE

The amount of ease allowed on most commercial patterns for pull-on skirts or slacks, is far too much. Check your pattern with a few measurements before cutting. Two inches (5cm) more than your waist measurement will give a fairly flat finish at the waist. Four inches (10cm) gives a slightly gathered look. Unless it is a very light weight knit and you wish a full effect, more than 4 inches (10cm) is excessive. Most of the commercial patterns carry straight up from the hips. This is necessary for a woven fabric to allow garment over your hips, but with knits, the fabric "gives" and it is not necessary to build in as much fullness. You may taper the side seam up to the waist as illustrated at right.

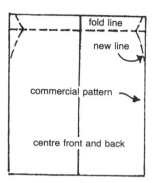

TRY ON PATTERN

Pin pattern tissue together, seam to seam and slip on. Tucks and adjustments are made much easier on paper prior to pattern cutting. Follow any of your pattern firms' sewing books on basic fitting techniques. Most newer patterns have adjustment instructions printed for you on the pattern.

Serger Fit Tip – See page 72.

Layout and Cutting

JIFFY "KNIT KNOW HOW"

- **Pre-shrink fabric** (see page 18).

hang fabric

- **Heavy stretch knits** such as velour, sweater knits etc., should be hung over rounded hanger for 24 hours prior to cutting, in order to stretch out as they will when hanging on the body.

- Always use **straight of grain** on one-way stretch fabrics with maximum stretch **around** the body.

- Can't tell the **right side**? Pull fabric across the grain as most knits will roll to the right side, especially single knits.

- **Follow pattern layouts**. Most knits are in 60 inch or 150cm widths.

- **Eliminate seams** where possible. Front and back seams can be cut on the fold. Cut the front facing of a dress or suit all in one with the front of garment. This gives less bulk and a smooth edge. This technique is usually only suitable for straight edges and requires a bit more fabric. The final result is worth it in your professionally finished garment.

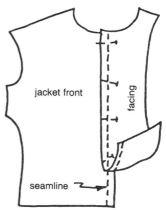

jacket front

facing

seamline

UNLINED JACKETS

If a jacket is to be unlined, it gives body through the upper part of the garment as well as a pleasing appearance to cut the facings as shown. This means you will trace off a pattern for them from the jacket pattern itself. Cut the front facing below the bust line and the back below the shoulder blade.

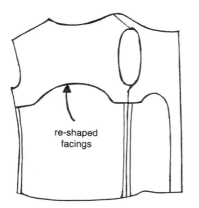

re-shaped facings

Sew shoulder seams right sides together (pressed open straight seam best here) on both garment and facings. Stitch underarm seam on facing also. Apply collar to neck edge at this point, then place right sides together, facings and garment. Stitch fronts and neck edge. Trim, turn and press. Place shoulder pad between facing and garment. With hand stitches, secure shoulder pad and facing edges to armhole.

SLEEVES

Most woven fabrics require a good cap in order to have enough ease through sleeve top. If you are using a commercial pattern, this may be excessive, when a knit is used. **Adjust easily by removing** ½" (1.3cm) to 1" (2.5cm) off cap top on pattern tapering to nothing 2 inches (5cm) above the notches. Amount to be removed depends

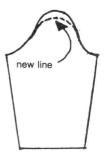

new line

on original cap height. When using shoulder pads approximately ½" (1.3cm) should be an adequate amount for removal.

SLEEVE CAP FILLER

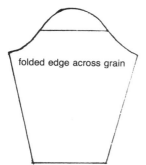

folded edge across grain

When the set-in sleeve is sewn in place on some knits, the seam allowance will sometimes show through giving a lumpy appearance. This can be rounded out and smoothed by addition of a bias cut strip approximately 1½" (3.8cm) (or crossgrain with a knit) across the cap top approximately 6 inches (15.3cm) in length. On a lighter weight fabric you can cut the strip double with the folded edge into the sleeve as shown here. Use the sleeve pattern for cutting the shape. Begin stitching bias strip where you have the greatest seam ease in sleeve cap and stretch very lightly as you sew. Match edge (or two edges if doubled) of bias strip to sleeve seam edges. Use a longer machine basting stitch, stitching as close as possible to sleeve seam stitching. Always turn the armhole seam allowance into sleeve.

CUTTING CORNERS

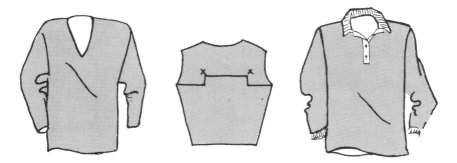

Different shaped yokes may be cut on your pattern and seam allowances added. Use contrasting coloured fabrics for interest, keeping fabric types similar. Stitch pieces together, but first...re-inforce the corners using the following methods:

I. Place pre-shrunk organdy or polyester organza on the garment right side, covering inside corner 2″ (5cm) all around. Stitch a ⅝″ (1.5cm) seam line around corner, (use short machine stitches) ensuring your needle is down as you pivot the corners.

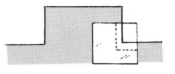

SEWN IN

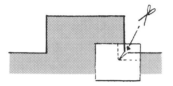

CUTTING LINE

2. Stopping at stitching line, slash through seam allowance into corner.

3. Turn organza piece to wrong side and press flat.

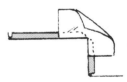

FOLD AND PRESS

SEW FROM CORNER

4. To join yoke to garment, begin stitching at corner point, sewing with regular seam to garment edge. Return to point and sew in opposite direction. This is excellent for use at tab front bottom, V-neck with set in piece or any other decorative square corners.

Note: Topstitching is attractive to highlight a seaming detail. To prevent a dip in topstitching, cut a small piece of angled fabric to fit corner in area where there is no seam allowance. Use a doublefaced fusible web to apply on the wrong side.

PATTERN PREPARATION

Press all pattern pieces with a warm dry iron. If using multiple sized pattern, trace the pattern onto one of the pattern tracing cloths available from your fabric store. See page 31 bottom of Interfacing Chart for suggestions.

Another idea for preserving your favourite patterns is to take the commercial pattern itself and press on a non-woven fusible interfacing. This method retains all the pattern markings and numbers. Tracing cloth or the interfacing both stick to knit fabrics which makes layout and cutting much easier.

CUTTING BOARD

These are made of cardboard and are marked with inches (centimetres) in each direction to provide for accurate placement of fabric on true grain in all directions. Fabric will not slide on this surface. Long, glass-headed pins will stick into the board holding your pattern pieces firmly in place. On firmer type double knits, cutting double and placing the pins perpendicular to edge works well. For T-shirt and softer knits (which don't lift completely when you cut) weights may be used. Glass furniture castors, ash trays, etc. are great and easy to use.

The board may be secured to a tabletop if you have a sewing room or be folded for easy storage. They are very inexpensive and can extend your cutting area. (6ft x 3ft /182cm x 91.5cm)

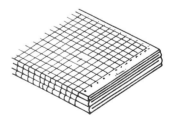

Note! Do not allow fabric to hang over the edge while cutting!

STRIPES

Cut stripes **single** thickness. This is made easier by tracing off a full front or full back as flipping the pattern over is not nearly as accurate. This is more time consuming but the effort is more

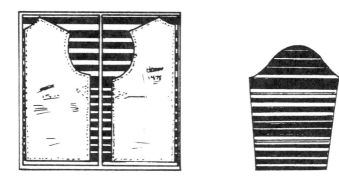

reliable in achieving stripes that match perfectly. The same position of stripe falls at the underarm (provided no dart) and the bottom of garment, front and back. The sleeve underarm will key up to the same stripe as well. The easiest stripe for layout is an even horizontal. Position the bottom hemline on dominant stripe for all pieces. Ensure the center stripes on front and back (if seam) match. Stripe should match from bustline down to hem. A slight mis-match will be hidden by arm from bustline upwards.

Horizontal uneven stripes are laid out in essentially the same manner as even stripes providing you use the "with-nap" directions or have the pattern pieces running in the same direction.

VARIATIONS

Using **stripe direction** for design effect can be very attractive. A dropped shoulder style dress looks very chic with the body of the dress running vertically and the sleeves horizontal, or the reverse. This is suitable for fairly firm knits as the vertical stripes may have a tendency to stretch.

Bias or Diagonal stripes give a flattering slimming effect to the figure. Cut a top on the bias. Use a regular facing, cutting it on the straight grain, running parallel to selvedge. This can be cut from a plain knit such as interlock. The cap sleeve or extended shoulder can be turned under and top

BIAS TOP

stitched. If you wish to have sleeves, try putting them on the bias and the garment body on the horizontal or vertical.

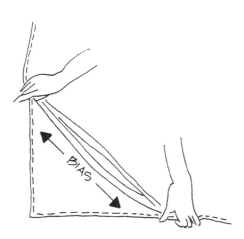

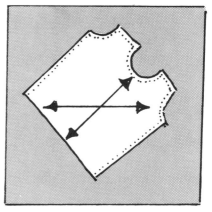

SELVEDGE

BIAS PLACEMENT

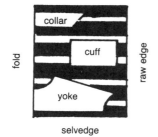

Collars, cuffs and yokes with stripes cut in opposite direction to garment give an interesting look.

MARKING

Use a marking pen or pencil to mark the wrong side of fabric that is difficult to distinguish. "Scotch Magic Tape"™ works well for marking knits. Use it to denote the right or wrong side of fabric, centre markings, etc.

Water Soluble Pens or Invisible Markers — Check your fabric to ensure that the marks will come out with water or evaporate in 48 hours. Choose a colour which is not too much of a contrast. It is wise to sew darts right away if using the evaporating type marker.

INTERLOCK KNITS

This fabric runs in one direction. Determine direction by pulling either end of yardage on the crosswise grain. Position pattern so your hemlines run upward.

TUBULAR FABRIC

Cut fabric apart prior to garment cutting. Occasionally a crease line remains on fabric fold. **Never use this as center** front or back as it may not fade out with washing. Tubular ribbed knits for sweaters or tube type skirts can be left uncut if the width is suitable for your size. If you wish the fabric to hug the body you will need to stretch it out the way you wish it to fit you. See Ribbing Page 50.

SCISSORS — See Page 23 Notions

ROTARY CUTTERS

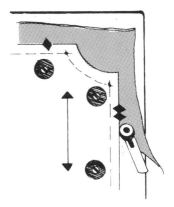

If using a Rotary Cutter, place a clear see-through plastic (metal dulls blade) ruler beside long straight edges. Ensure that you have cutting surface beneath. Weights may be used as there is no fabric or pattern movement with this method.

Sewing Knits

CONVENTIONAL SEWING MACHINE

Knits can be sewn on any machine, even grandmother's old treadle! However, some of the new machines have marvellous built-in stretch stitches which help to make your finished garment more attractive and durable.

GUIDELINES FOR TROUBLE FREE SEWING

- **Regulate I2 stitches per inch** or less.

- **Reduce pressure** of presser foot, dependent on machine. If seam ripples or puckers, adjust the tension as required. A longer stitch may sew better when working with looser knits.

- **Ease** the fabric by use of roller foot attachment which keeps the top fabric from edging ahead of the lower piece.

  roller foot

- **Even Feed Foot** — Separate attachments are available to fit most machines including straight or slant needle types. These are more sophisticated than the roller foot and take care of most puckering on light weight knits, as well as seam edges extending following stitching. On some machines this is a built-in feature called a "match-maker" or "dual-feed" foot and is clicked into place with one press of your finger.

CORRECT TENSION

TOP TENSION TOO TIGHT   BOTTOM TENSION TOO TIGHT

- **Tension** — Your seam could snap if tension is improperly adjusted. Stretching fabric while sewing is generally unnecessary as a well stitched seam contains enough elasticity in itself. One exception would be silky jersey where pulling front and back of fabric (taut sewing) while sewing, generally gives a smooth seam.

Knit Tip: Keep two bobbin cases, one for knits which is looser, and a tighter one for use with woven fabrics.

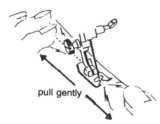

pull gently

- **Curved areas** (armholes, crotch seams) may be slightly stretched when sewing as stress factor is high in these areas. Use of high density stretch stitches would be desirable here as well.

- When **starting your seam**, pull your threads from the back which helps eliminate possibility of them going down into the race. Many knits are soft and have this tendency.

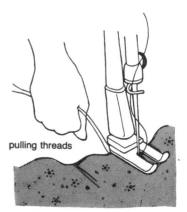

pulling threads

Overlock Serger machines are now available to the homesewer. If you have never used one, avail yourself of a demonstration at your sewing department or machine dealer. We cover, in depth all the information needed to make your serger sewing with knits more enjoyable. Refer to chapters 12 & 13 specifically, with many others giving serging tips.

Seam Finishes

CONVENTIONAL MACHINES

The type of seam used to finish a garment will depend on the type of care the garment will have later (washing or drycleaning) and whether the seams will be shown during wearing.

PLAIN SEAM

Generally a ⅝″ (1.5cm) seam allowance, sewn with straight stitch and pressed open. This is suitable for wool or polyester double knits and heavier fabrics where a less bulky, flat seam allowance is desired. For appearance, a second row of straight stitching, zig-zag or step zig-zag can be sewn along edges of seam allowance.

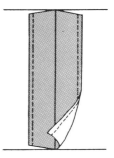

DOUBLE-STITCHED SEAM

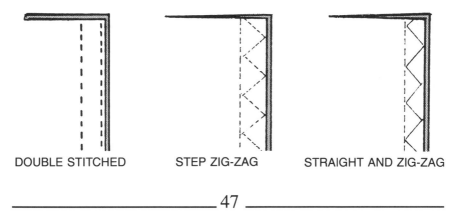

DOUBLE STITCHED   STEP ZIG-ZAG   STRAIGHT AND ZIG-ZAG

A strong, narrow stretchy variation of the plain seam. Use this method for soft single knits such as jersey to minimize raw edges curling. Use on sweater knits and terry to control ravelling. Also suitable for plush knits such as velour and stretch terry, as seam allowances are trimmed to reduce bulk. To construct, make a plain seam and stitch again ¼" (6 mm) away from first stitch. Trim seam allowance close to second stitching. If you have a regular or multiple serpentine zig-zag, use this for second row of stitching. The combination straight stitch and zig-zag is best as use of zig-zag by itself gives a gappy seam when pressed, although it retains more elasticity.

NARROW ZIG-ZAG SEAM

A very tiny zig-zag by itself is used one row on lingerie or two rows on two-way stretch fabrics, one tiny and one larger. For lingerie, trim seam back close to stitching. Tiny seam edges will roll back almost covering seam. A nice finish!

NARROW
ZIG-ZAG

WITH LARGER
ZIG-ZAG

EDGE OVERCAST OR OVERLOCK STRETCH STITCH

This is a built-in reverse action stitch on many machines. It offers a multiple stretch stitch and overcast all in one motion. This is fantastic for swimwear, bodysuits and close fitting garments giving a great deal of stretch. **Caution!** Make sure your garment fits! These stitches are difficult to remove if you sew in error.

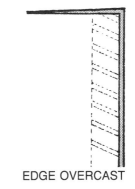

EDGE OVERCAST

TAPING SEAMS

¼″ (6mm) (preshrunk) twill tape
or seam binding may be used at
shoulder seams, necklines, yoke
seams, front closings and pocket
openings where the stretch should
be limited for retention and long
wear. Cut tape the length shown
on pattern piece and pin in place,
stitching into the seam as you sew.
Light T-shirt fabrics generally do

TAPING SEAM

not require taping but a heavier, looser type may need taping even
on armhole seams in addition to shoulders. Heavy Coat knits would
be another garment needing taping.

STAY STITCHING

Generally unnecessary except with very loose knits where it is
advisable on neck and armhole edges as well as shoulders. It is
important to stay stitch neck edges where a collar will be applied if
using a serger. You can then clip along neckline to the stitching
allowing the seam line to lay straight for sewing. See page 92.

TURNING EDGES UNDER

This is not advisable on knits as it causes ridges due to bulk of the
fabric. Finish facing edges, hems, with a fancy stitch on your
machine or sheer tricot bias seams finish (see page 23). Occasionally
facing and neck edges on a tab front or neck opening will have
edges turned under, but only on the light weight knits. Knit fabrics,
contrary to convention, do not ravel on the vertical grain.

OVERLOCK SERGING seams are covered in Chapter 12.

Ribbed and Self Trim

Ribbed trim has been popular for sportswear for many years as it fits snugly without binding and looks attractive. However, in recent years there are many more uses for regular complete garments such as "tube" skirts, waistbands, inserts in shirts, tights, turtleneck shirts, etc. If using rib-knit for a complete garment the sizing of your pattern will need to be adjusted or purchase one that is styled for that type of knit. However, if you wish to use a **regular pattern** the following is a method which will work.   This is meant to be a body-hugging look!

TUBE AND RIB KNIT SKIRTS, DRESSES, SWEATERS

Using a padded surface, stretch your fabric out crosswise the desired amount you wish it to be stretched on your body. Stick pins down each side at intervals of 3 to 4 inches (7.5cm to 10cm). Place pattern on and pin parallel to the pattern edge every inch or two (2.5 or 5cm). This step is very important, using many pins to hold pattern in place, as the fabric will spring back to it's original unstretched state with the first cut into the fabric. When cut, your garment piece will look rather small and somewhat distorted in shape. However, when it is sewn and put on the body it will look like the original design. Manufacturers would draft a pattern to the size needed for the fabric, however, this is a method for the homesewer that works quite satisfactorily when a regular pattern is used.

> SELF TRIM *may be pieced together. If necessary join on the bias to give less bulk in seam and make join at the back or inconspicuous place before sewing.*

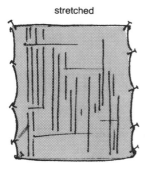

stretched

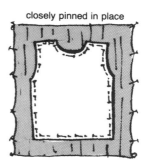

closely pinned in place

CUT RIB TRIM

MEASUREMENT OF HEADBAND

Cut long enough to fit snugly around waist, ankle or wrist, adding seam allowances to both ends. To measure for a crew neck finish, pull the band (fold in half) around your head snugly. The width will be double the desired finished width plus seam allowances. For example 2″ (5cm) finished cuff would be 4" **plus** seam allowances. Refer to page 54.

If using elastic at a waistband, as well as the ribbing it is not necessary to stretch the ribbing excessively. It is recommended that elastic be placed inside the ribbing as it will hold better. In order to eliminate a lot of fullness at the waistline, ribbing is sometimes used for a distance of 4 to 5 inches (10 to 12.7cm) from the top. This is an ideal finish for maternity skirts and slacks.

SELF FABRIC TRIM

Some fabrics such as velour, stretch terry, and some doubleknits have enough cross grain stretch to use the self fabric method.

SHIRRED
ELASTIC CUFF

If fabric isn't moderately stretchy you may use approximately 4″ (10cm) more than wrist or ankle measurements and topstitch . Ensure opening is left to thread elastic through. As a waistline or cuff technique you could use three rows of ½″(1.3cm) elastic. This is often used for a decorative touch as well.

Chanel or Self Trim

This finish is ideal for garments where you want a dressier look. Width of finished trim is your decision, but generally a ½″ (1.3cm) finished width is customary. Use the garment self fabric or a contrast if desired. This can be used for neck, sleeve or center front edge trim. For use as trim around an outside corner refer to one of the basic sewing books (available locally) for the instructions on how to mitre.

1. For a ½″ (1.3cm) finished trim, cut a 2″ (5cm) wide bias strip by desired length, or if fabric has enough stretch, cut a straight piece across the grain.

2. Place against neck edge with right sides together, bias strip extended beyond center back seam ½″ (1.3cm) approximately. The seam allowance width will determine the finished chanel trim width. Sew using a regular machine stitch, gently stretching banding into curved areas as you sew. Turn bias to back side, tucking in ends at center back, and pin in place.

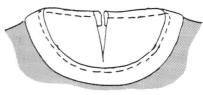

IN PLACE

3. Return to front side and stitch in welt formed by turning over fabric to wrong side. If your thread is a **perfect match** your stitches will be almost invisible.

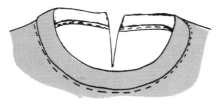

FOLD BACK AND STITCH

4. Press trim toward the stitching as this will further hide your stitches.

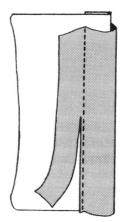

5. Trim back side of trim to within ⅛ inch (3mm) of stitching line. Fray check may be applied to this edge, if heavy wear or fraying is a possibility. Knit trim may be sewn to any fabric in this manner. Light weight leather, synthetic suede etc., may be substituted for self fabric with this method. A slightly wider finish may be desired for a pocket top edging.

When using this method for a **high neck**, a **zipper** must be applied at neck as there is not adequate stretch for clearance unless neckline itself is lower. If zipper is required, install **prior** to finishing neck edge with self trim. You will need trim slightly stretched into curve on a scoop type neckline to ensure trim hugs in nicely. See page 102, Zippers.

Armseye Trim

Self-trim may be applied to sleeveless armhole edges in similar manner. For ribbing trim, ⅔ or ¾ of armhole measurement will suffice. For self-trim, put in place by dividing in half, putting most stretch while sewing in underarm areas.

RUFFLED RIBBING (Lettuce edging)

This presents a dainty finish for a little girl's T-shirt. Cut double the depth normally cut as this will be folded over banding. For example an 8″ (20.3cm) depth will yield a 2″ (5cm) finished depth when completed. This gives a turtle neck appearance.

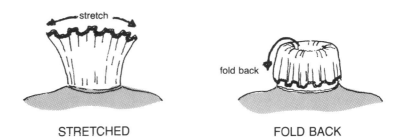

STRETCHED   FOLD BACK

Use this also for cuff treatments. Sew neckband to the neck using the basic T-shirt method, page 85. To create a ruffle, set your machine at a medium to wide zig-zag stitch with a short stitch length. Sew on folded edge of ribbing, stretching as much as possible while sewing. More than one row of stitching may be necessary. A "fluted" effect will occur. This same idea could be used on the bottom of a velour robe to present a very feminine look. Use a piece of scrap material for your experimentation before sewing your garment. If using a stretchy fabric for a casual type lounge dress, you may want to try this for the hem or sleeves.

MAKEOVERS

Are there sweaters in your family that are out of style? It is very easy to re-cut and style them into "new" sweaters. Even men's sweaters can be made over. Shorten length, stay-stitch and then re-apply the banding.

If you do not have enough knit for a complete garment, you may add leather pieces, hand knit sleeves or even woven fabrics in combinations of your choosing. See Sweater Chapter page 91.

Overlock Serging Machines

In keeping with the innovative 80's we as homesewers are now able to maintain pace with manufacturing techniques available to us in the form of serging machines. These powerful little machines will sew up to 1700 stitches per minute, almost twice the speed of a regular machine. **They not only stitch but will trim and overcast all in ONE efficient operation.** To sew your garments in half the usual time, gives renewed interest in sewing to many half-hearted seamstresses, as well as enabling advanced sewers to produce many more professionally finished garments. Have you often wished you could finish your seams as in store bought garments? Now you

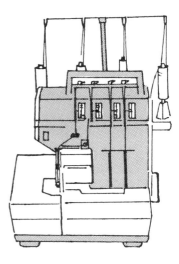

can! Manufacturers have several different machines to do the work that homesewers are hoping to accomplish with one. In the process, some of the finished products have the "loving hands-at-home" look. You need to consider this prior to sewing your garment. **Do I want to sew everything on the serger?** Except for the "10 minute dress", the answer is definitely **"no"**. **You will want to use your conventional sewing machine in conjunction with your serger.** Zippers, buttonholes, topstitching and standard seams must be stitched on a conventional machine.

These machines are excellent for knits as the stitches are neat but very stretchy, while at the same time the seams do not get overstretched in the sewing. Several of the overlock machines on the market have a "differential feed mechanism". This prevents puckering and/or stretching of woven and/or knitted fabric. This is one more adjustment to be made when changing fabrics, but if you want fine tuning this feature is available.

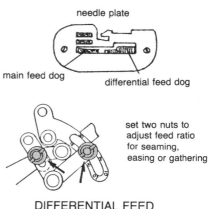

needle plate

main feed dog

differential feed dog

set two nuts to
adjust feed ratio
for seaming,
easing or gathering

DIFFERENTIAL FEED

Each machine has it's own special features. Some have snap-on feet, swing-out feet, built-in rolled hemmers (no need to change feet or plates), dials to adjust stitch length (no screw driver needed!), colour-coded threading, built-in waist containers, lights, accessory storage or blade finger-guards. In factories a machine can be set up for a long run on a particular fabric and there is no need to change the settings. The above features have been specially geared to the homesewer in order to assist her in making easy adjustments for the stitches required to complete a garment. Once you have mastered the threading, tension adjustments and general operation of an overlock machine you will wonder how you ever sewed without one!

TYPES OF OVERLOCK SERGERS

There are several basic types of overlock machines for specific needs. You need to decide which type of sewing you will be doing most, prior to making your purchase. In the last couple of years there have been changes almost every month, with new models streamlining this market.

Overlock sergers fall into four categories, depending on the number of threads and needles they use. There are many combinations of these, the most recent being a 2/3/4-thread all in one machine. It would be a machine that a person with serger experience could enjoy.

TWO THREAD SERGER

This machine is considered to be an over-edge serger. This is primarily used to trim and overcast raw edges. The edges are much less bulky with the use of two threads. Serging can be done prior to assembling garment pieces together. The threads do not lock at the seam line, thus this is **not a stitch used for stitching**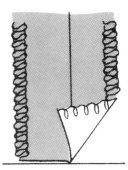
seams together. "Flatlocking" as it is sometimes called, is most effective with a two-thread overlock although it is possible with a three thread (seam will not lay as flat). See page 77.

THREE THREAD OVERLOCK

This machine is an overlock stitching serger using three threads.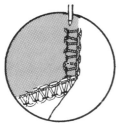
The stitches formed by this machine lock at the seamline and have a nearly identical appearance on both sides. It can be used to cut, finish and sew seams, giving an elastic stitch very suitable for knits and garments needing some ease. Bias cut garments fit into this category. There are several features that vary from machine to machine including, flat locking, some convert to a two-stitch over-edge finish if desired, others will stitch a tiny rolled hem with or without changing the throat plate. See page 74.(rolled edges) The three thread is probably the most versatile machine for the homesewer, especially if it has the two thread combination.

THREE/FOUR THREAD OVERLOCK

This machine will basically stitch the same as the three-thread but adds an additional row of straight stitching down the middle, for added strength. This is formed by a second needle which runs parallel to the first, similar to a twin needle. It has almost as much stretch to the stitch as the straight three-thread. This heavier stitching is not required for over-edge finishing, therefore it is possible to remove one of the 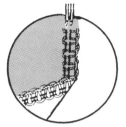 needles to give a lighter finish. By threading either the right or left needle on a three-thread stitch you can achieve a wider or narrower stitch width. This machine cannot convert to a two-thread over-edge, but it will do a rolled hem. The left needle will need to be removed to do a narrow rolled edge. Even though you do not thread the needle, your stitches will not form properly if you leave the needle in place. See page 74, Rolled Edges.

TRUE FOUR THREAD OVERLOCK

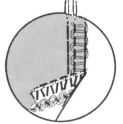 Seam finishing for easily ravelled fabrics is simplified with this machine. All four threads are required to form a seam. The chain formed by two threads, and an overedge stitch with the other two threads, produces a very strong stitch. It is possible to drop the right needle and obtain a straight chain stitch or drop the left needle to create a two thread overedge stitch. This complete four-thread stitching is very stable and thus suited to fabrics and areas where you wish to maintain the shape (shoulder seams, armholes, etc.) It is not suitable for garments where stretch is necessary, as the **seam has no elasticity!** It is not possible to do a rolled edge with this machine.

HOW DOES AN OVERLOCK SERGER WORK?

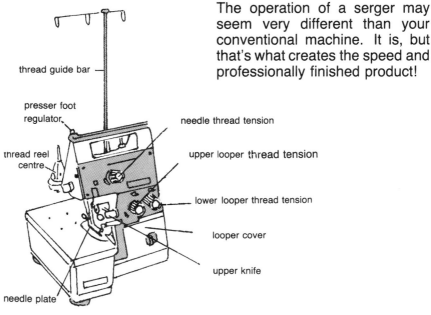

The operation of a serger may seem very different than your conventional machine. It is, but that's what creates the speed and professionally finished product!

thread guide bar

presser foot regulator

thread reel centre

needle thread tension

upper looper thread tension

lower looper thread tension

looper cover

upper knife

needle plate

KNIVES

There are two blades, an upper and a lower blade, which cut or trim the edge of the seam allowance. One is made of a harder steel than the other. If desired, on most machines (check this), **the upper blade can be rotated out of the way** for changing needles, stitching the last stitches to complete a circle,

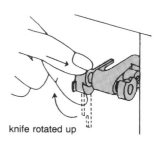

knife rotated up

enabling you to see more clearly and not cut the edge. The blades will usually stay sharp for a long time. However, should you run into a pin it will be necessary to change the blade. The bottom blade will probably need to be replaced first. Instructions for doing this are in your machine booklet.

LOOPERS

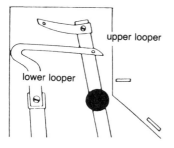

The upper and lower loopers are below the throatplate of the machine and along with needle threads combine to form the overlock stitch. There are no bobbins on these machines, thus it is possible to run off a chain with no fabric in the machine.

PRESSER FOOT

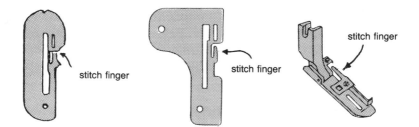

Overlock stitches are formed over the stitch finger (former) which is a "prong" found on the throat plate or presser foot, depending on the brand of machine. See Stitch Width page 66.

The presser foot is considerably longer on an overlock machine and does not need to be lifted at the beginning and end of a seam as in conventional sewing. See page 82, Continuous Sewing.

SKIPPED STITCHES: *A Stretch (ball point) or Blue needle will sometimes build up resin on the needle tip which causes skipping problems. Clean tip of needle with alcohol. A finer size will also correct the problem on occasion.*

The **Presser Foot Regulator** (pressure) is a knob usually on the top of the machine which is either screwed down; right to tighten or left to loosen. Some are like a button that you push to tighten or loosen. The only times that adjustment may be necessary is to tighten for heavy fabrics and loosen for light ones.

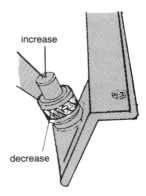

increase

decrease

TENSION REGULATORS

Unlike conventional machines, the tension knobs or regulators will be adjusted **constantly** as you change stitch length, width or thread, for various applications. At first this will seem somewhat complicated, but as you begin to understand how a well balanced stitch looks, you will immediately know which tension regulator to adjust. Each machine varies as to the type of regulator it may have. Most have numbers on them, some rotate only once, some twice, while others may go around many times. On occasion it is necessary to wrap your thread around a disc a couple of times to get the desired tension. This is especially true when doing a narrow rolled hem where the lower looper tension needs to be very tight to pull the upper thread over to make the roll.

> *Serger Tip:* An easy way to get the loopers threads sorted out, is to remember that the **top looping thread** (as you are sewing) is the "upper" or right looper and the **underneath looping thread** is the "lower" or left looper with the straight stitch on top inner part of seam being the needle thread. This would depict a typical three thread stitch.

SERGING THREAD

Cross-wound thread is desired for sergers. Because the threads are reeled upwards to the thread guides (the cone does not move) they can pull very quickly with the high speed. Use adapters or cone holders provided with your machine. Some larger tube type threads will not need the adapters.

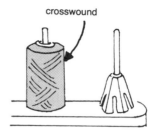

crosswound

Parallel-wound thread is used for conventional sewing machines as the thread comes off the spool from the side. However, if you need to use regular sewing machine thread for colour, place the spool with the notch down and a spool cap (also provided) over the top of spool. These are larger than your spool, purposely so that the thread does not catch the top of spool but winds off freely.

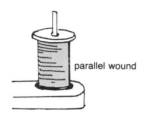

parallel wound

An extra fine thread is required for serging in that with two, three or four layers of thread stitched together, a very heavy seam would result with regular thread. Most major thread companies are now producing special thread for the homesewing, serger market. Some are 100% polyester while others are polyester core with a cotton wrap. Because sergers operate at high speed, the thread must be strong. One process even burns the "fuzzies" off, retaining a high sheen on the finished thread. One of the newest, versatile types of thread, especially for knits is the "Woolley Lock" nylon thread. See Page 19, Notions.

Because of the speed and numbers of threads, you will require larger cones of thread. Purchasing a large cone does not necessarily mean you will get a fine quality thread. As a matter of fact some of the larger cones have the poorest quality threads! Because of the larger put-up, the large cones are generally cheaper in price.

As you will be sewing some steps with your conventional machine, keep in mind that you will need an extra spool with the same colour thread for that purpose.

It is possible to **use several different qualities** of thread for one seam. For example try a stretchy nylon in the lower looper, regular polyester in the needle and perle cotton No. 8 in the upper looper. This makes a very nice combination for finishing placemats, or the edge of a heavier jacket fabric.

> *Serger Tip:* Watch that you are actually getting a finer thread on the larger spools as some companies are using their regular thread for this put-up.

WHAT COLOUR SHOULD I CHOOSE FOR SERGING?

Purchase neutral colours, ivory, beige, black, grey, etc., (one cone per spool holder), as in most cases serged seams are on the inside. Matching colours can be used if preferred, especially when using the serge stitch on the outside of the garment, but it can be rather costly. The most important thread to **colour match is the needle thread**, as it will sometimes show on the right side.

Decorative Overlock Stitching — see page 79.

TIPS ON THREADING

* *Always leave the machine threaded* as threading the loopers is a bit tricky. When a change of colour is necessary, just snip the threads at the spools and tie on new threads, using an overhand knot.

> *Serger Tip:* Pulling the looper threads through, prior to threading the needle, seems to eliminate the possibility of the threads breaking.

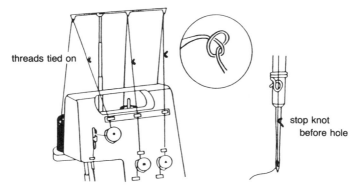

threads tied on

stop knot before hole

- *Raise upper knife to simplify needle threading.*

- *Disengage thread from needle(s).*

- *Loosen looper tension discs,* to allow knots to pass through easily, or pop thread out of dials, and run machine while gently pulling both threads from behind presser foot till the knots are through the machine. Check threads in looper tension discs, ensuring that the new thread is engaged correctly.

- *Manually pull thread through needle tension disc(s),* or thread needle(s) and run machine till knot is at needle. Snip knot and re-thread needles. These threads can be pulled back but laid on top of presser foot back.

Thread Cradle can be made by wrapping regular thread around heavier yarn or "wooley nylon". This enables easy threading through looper. If it won't pull through, the yarn is too thick.

STITCH LENGTH AND WIDTH REGULATORS

Stitch Length — can be regulated from 1mm to 5mm depending on the type of machine. Some machines have screws on the lower left inside which are adjusted with a screwdriver to the

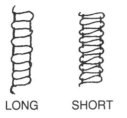

LONG   SHORT

desired length. Others have dials, and still others can be moved with settings on the handwheel. Your desired seam or finish will determine the length you should use. Decorative work will require a close stitch, where overedge finishing should be open or longer.

Stitch Width — can be regulated from 1 to 7mm depending on the brand of machine. The narrowest finish would be the rolled edge, where you would either change the presser foot or throat plate of the machine. The width of the "stitch finger" (prong) helps to determine the stitch width.

WIDE   NARROW

Removing the left needle will make your stitch narrower. (possible on 3/4 thread machines only.)

Move lower knife — Turn upper knife out of way, in highest position. Loosen lower knife, usually by turning screw. Adjust for narrower seam width by moving knife to the left and to widen seam slide it to the right. Follow machine instruction book.

Move dial to desired width — This is a convenient feature on some machines in that you can set the dial to a desired number width.

Generally the widest stitching is desirable for decorative stitches where the use of heavier crochet thread or yarn is used. It gives a smart professional look. Experiment till you like the look!

OVERLOCK TIP: *DO NOT USE 3-in-one oil on sergers. It will gum up the machine. Use only sewing machine oil.*

NEEDLES

Many of the overlock machines use regular conventional machine needles. These you would place in machine with flat of needle at top back. However, many still use industrial needles which are more sturdy and last longer. They do come in several sizes, including ballpoint. Many of the skipping problems are reduced with sergers. However, if skipping does occur, ensure fabric has been pre-washed, removing any sizing or resins, and needle is not dull, before inserting a ballpoint needle. Nylon lycra with high density of stitches would be one fabric where a needle change may be necessary. See page 21, Notions. Change your needle size in accordance with weight of fabric. Raising upper knife makes needle change much easier.

The overlock industrial needles have a round shank with a long groove in front and a "scarf" which is placed at the back. The **needle eye must face front**. Tweezers (usually supplied with the accessory kit for the machine) simplify insertion. Most of the overlock machines using two needles have two separate screws. However, should you have only one screw for both, the tweezers will defini- 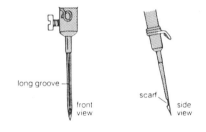 tely aid in the process of changing a needle. **If a needle is incorrectly placed, the machine will not stitch properly.** Industrial needles form a better stitch.

OVERLOCK SERGING NOTIONS

Extra Long Tweezers — are the ideal tool for inserting and threading needles and loopers. Shorter tweezers usually come in your machine kit, but the extra long ones are even better.

Canned Air — A must for an Overlock Serger owner! There are several brands available. This aerosol container shoots pressurized air into those difficult places where lint collects. It comes in a small, pocket container, or cans where you can purchase a nozzle which can be put onto refill cans.

Rubber Foot Mat — This mat keeps the foot pedal from sliding around the floor. Helps ease the frustration!

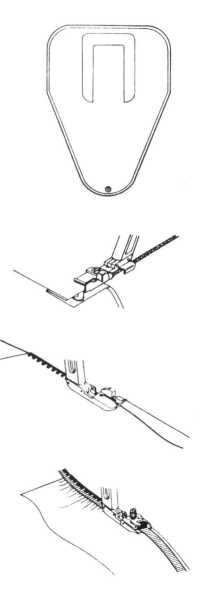

Blind Hemming Foot or Decorative Stitch Guide — This foot is only available with some machines. Lengthen stitch to longest length; loosen the tension so you just barely catch thread of garment.

Cording Foot — This foot is only available with some machines. It holds the cord in position while overlocking. This method can be used to stabilize seams such as shoulder seams in knits and loosely woven fabrics.

Elastic Foot — This also is only available with some machines. It has a roller and tension control which eliminates the need to stretch the elastic. Elastic is inserted into foot which automatically guides it for even application. Usually it has a set narrow width and only elastics of that size can be used.

Wonder Tape — This wash-a-way Wonder Tape, completely disappears in first washing. See page 71.

Sewing It Up With A Serger

For preparation, read chapters 3, Fabric Preparation, 7, Fast Fitting Tips, and 8, Layout and Cutting.

Prior to sewing you will need to stitch a few sample stitches to ensure that the tension is correct for your particular fabric. It is easier to have one long strip so that you can continue while adjusting each regulator as needed. When beginning to learn it is advisable to put different colours of thread on each thread reel in order to quickly identify where to correct the problems. A well stitched seam should not look like a "ladder" when pulled apart. With knit fabrics it is advisable to leave short loops on the edge of seam. These are reduced when the fabric stretches in wearing.

Thread tension is adjusted by moving your tension regulators on the face of the overlock machine. See page 62. Turn the regulators **Right to tighten, Left to loosen**. Memorize the two steps and you will have no hesitation when correction is needed.

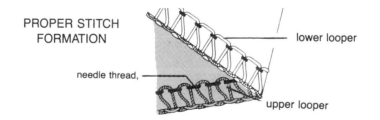

PROPER STITCH FORMATION

lower looper

needle thread,

upper looper

1. **Needle tension is too loose, or upper right or lower (Left) looper thread tensions are too tight.** Correction: Increase needle thread tension, or decrease the upper (right) or lower (left) looper thread tensions.

2. **Upper (Right) looper thread tension is too loose, or the lower (Left) looper thread tension is too tight.** Correction: Increase the upper (right) looper thread tension, or decrease the lower (left) looper thread tension.

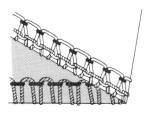

3. **Lower (Left) looper thread tension is too loose, or the upper (Right) looper thread tension is too tight.** Correction: Increase the lower (left) looper thread tension, or decrease the upper (right) tension.

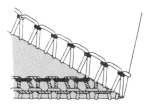

HOLDING SEAMS TOGETHER

PIN PARALLEL

1. With conventional machines, pinning is usually done perpendicular to the edge, with the possibility of sewing over them. With serger sewing it is best to pin parallel to the edge approximately 1″ (2.5cm) away as your blades can be dulled and ruined quickly if they come into contact with a pin.

2. **Fabric Glue Stick** (water soluble) applied sparingly to slippery or striped fabrics, along seam allowance is another possibility. Place this along edge of seam allowance which will be cut off when serging.

3. **Wash-a-way tape** is a double sided transparent tape that can be stitched through. Unlike other tapes, it will not gum up your needle. It will completely disappear after first washing. Because the tape is water soluble, it should be stored in a cool dry place when not in use.

4. Machine or hand basting is still necessary as a last resort if using slippery or unusual fabric. However, this step gives a great opportunity for **fitting the garment** prior to final sewing!

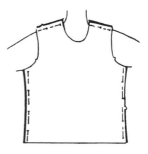

PIN FIT

SEAM GUIDE MARKINGS

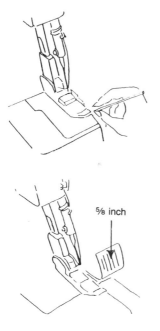

These are not usually on an overlock machine. You can mark them yourself with tape or a small dot of nail polish applied with a toothpick at the needle position on presser foot, ⅜″ (1cm) and ⅝″ (1.5cm) marks on upper knife guard. Measure your markings from the needle to the right. After awhile it becomes much easier to gauge distance required.

SEAMS

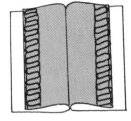

Decide ahead whether you wish a **regular straight seam with over-edge finishing** or **a stitched and cut overlock seam**. It is best to start with a ⅝" (1.5cm) seam allowance when serging a narrow seam, trimming off excess when stitching.

STITCHED AND CUT

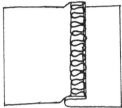

USE OVERLOCK SEAMS

- For lightweight single knit fabrics where edges roll.
- For "action wear" garments where strength and stretch is needed.
- For garments that will be laundered.
- When loosely woven/knitted fabric is used.
- When narrow seams are desired for sheer fabric.

USE COMBINATION SEAMS

- When a pressed open seam is desired for bulky heavy wovens/knits. (Over-edge serging on most knits would be for appearance only as they do not fray).
- For body-hugging styles where a flat seam gives less ridge.
- When placing a zipper, pocket in place.
- When there may be need to change seam later.
- For Lapped seams — edges serged and top-stitched in place.

- In **areas of stress**, crotch, armhole and neck seams, an additional row of straight stitching with conventional machine will strengthen. Children's clothing will wear better if you take this additional step.

- Double-stitched Seams where the seam is pressed to one side and top stitched.

ROLLED AND UNROLLED EDGES, NARROW SEAMS

This finish is one of the wonders available to us on the overlock machines. It is achieved by changing the throatplate or presser foot. The width of the stitch finger determines the width of the stitch.

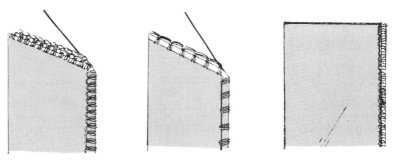

| short stitch length | longer stitch length | narrow seam |

Rolled Edges: **Loosen the upper looper tension and tighten the lower looper.** This pulls the upper looper thread over to back side and causes the fabric to roll. It may be necessary to wrap thread around the lower looper tension a couple of times to get the stitches pulling properly. Check the knife position if you find that the edge still doesn't roll over or has fibres sticking out. Another adjustment is to adjust presser foot pressure. The **stitch length** will cause the stitch to be either solid (satin type) or spaced apart. A two or three-thread **picot edge** is a rolled edge with longer stitch length. This is very nice on tricot or sheer fabrics, also veils.

Unrolled Edge: This is best used where the fabric is too bulky to roll. It gives a neat finish. Use a balanced stitch.

Ruffles can be sewn in minutes using these neat edges. Beautiful duplication of "French hand sewing" or Pintucking is extremely easy to accomplish. See page 123. A "lettuce" edge can be made by stretching in front of needle only, on two way stretch fabric or ribbing. See Ruffled Ribbing Page 54. An unrolled edge makes a beautiful seam in itself for sheer fabrics or laces. See page 123.

Spaghetti straps can be sewn quickly with a narrow seam on either a two or three thread serger.

1. Sew a chain (thread only, no fabric) approximately 4"(10cm) longer than the length of the strap, leaving chain on machine.

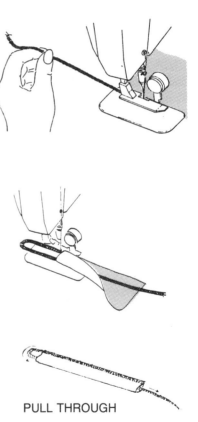

2. Bring thread chain around to front placing on right side of fabric piece as close to centre as possible. Fold fabric lengthwise so raw edges meet, placing needle in position with seam line.

3. Sew tube, cutting off excess seam allowance.

4. To turn tube, pull on the chain from the bottom. Continue pulling until entire chain is pulled through and tubing is right side out.

PULL THROUGH

If using a two thread stitch, you may pull seam apart (like flatlock seam) at this stage, and the seam will then be flat. Press tubing so that seam is at the centre.

A **loop turner** can also be used to turn a narrow seamed strap. Eliminate the long chain of thread, Steps 1 and 2. Poke turner to one end. Secure hook and pull through. If pulling a long tube, pressure is needed to keep the hook in place. Someone else can hold the ring at the end of the turner, or if you are alone, place one foot on the ring end and then you can maintain pressure while pulling with both hands.

LOOP TURNER

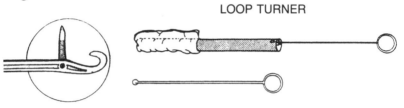

French Seams can also be done easily with the narrow unrolled edge. Refer to Silks 'N Satins book page 66, replacing first step with serging stitch.

LAPPED OVERLOCK SEAMS

This method works well with heavy fabrics. It is advisable to use one of the decorative types of thread or even ribbon (sew slow) on the outer edges. Regular thread is used in the needle and decorative threads in the loopers. The widest stitch gives the best look.

Consider the order in which you will be putting garment together, and the seams you wish to have on the outside.

1. Serge (with regular thread) all edges that will be inside. Generally all back garment edges, except for neck and armhole (if sleeveless), or yoke and centre seams.

2. Stabilize edges if required by using one of the techniques on page 92.

3. Serge lapping edges with decorative threads.

4. Lap seams together, holding in place with one of methods page 71. Topstitch together with conventional straight stitch machine, using two rows stitching, if desired.

MOCK FLATLOCK OR TRELLIS SEAM

Manufacturers have a special machine to produce a true flatlock seam. It is called a "Top and Bottom Cover Stitch" machine. This machine does not stitch on the edge of a seam, but stitches on the flat. It uses 5 or 6 threads and 3 or 4 needles producing a very strong stitch. Ready-to-wear has used it with wool jerseys in very couture looks.

However, homesewers can achieve a similar looking stitch. This is basically a two thread seam, **which is not meant as a holding seam, but rather an overedge stitch**. It does not have the overlock or third thread to give it strength. However for decorative purposes it can be very attractive. This stitch works most effectively on sweatshirt, interlock, velour, terry and double knits, using sportswear styles.

- Stitches can be used from either side. Flatlock has the heavier stitching on the outside and the Trellis side has a "ladder" appearance. Either side is effective, but the ladder side can give the appearance that your garment is coming apart!
- Often used on trendy sportswear, especially knit fabrics.
- Only suitable for fabrics that do not ravel.
- Pulling seam apart gives a very flat seam.

TWO THREAD FLATLOCK

for strength

Some three thread machines will convert to two threads and a four thread machine will convert to two threads by threading only the right needle and looper. As the stitch is created by an **unbalanced tension**, it may be necessary to loosen tensions in order to flatten seam following stitching.

No, the best

To have heavier loop stitching on right side, place wrong sides together. Sew two layers together; pull on the layers until seam is flat. Place right sides together for trellis stitch finish showing to garment right side.

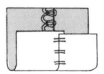

THREE THREAD FLATLOCK

It is possible to do a flatlock stitch with a three thread machine, but it will not lay as flat. Loosen the needle tension and tighten the lower looper tension until the lower loops disappear. Experiment with two thicknesses of fabric, adjusting tension till the seam will lay flat.

DECORATIVE FLATLOCK STITCHING

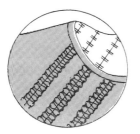

A form of **topstitching** can be done by folding fabric, wrong sides together at a desired spot, and flatlocking the edge (being careful not to cut fold). Pull the fabric apart. By adding several rows, horizontally or vertically, a decorative effect can be achieved. For more emphasis, use crochet cotton (No. 5 or 8), perle cotton, silky rayon or "Wooley nylon"™.

RELEASING STITCH FINGER THREADS

Because the stitches are formed over a "stitch finger" or prong, this is a necessary step to learn in order to free your stitches. Areas where this technique is required are as follows:

• Securing seam ends with overlock stitching, see below.

• Starting and finishing sewing at middle point of seam. This technique eliminates overlapping of stitches especially for placemats, napkins, and scarves.

• Turning corners without chaining off.

• Basically any time you wish to pull the threads, but leave stitching in place.

Serger Tip: When working with decorative threads it may be necessary to wind off a quantity on floor or put ball in bowl.

"Hiccups" will occur if yarn doesn't wind off freely.

STEPS FOR CLEARING

1. Lift needle to highest position.

2. Raise presser foot.

3. Pull needle thread from front, ever so slightly.

4. Pull stitches off finger from behind.

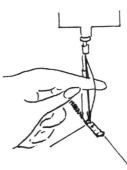

pull needle thread

SECURING SEAM ENDS

Starting with a 2″ (5cm) chain placed to the back of the machine, stitch seam and run off another 4″ (10cm). **If seams will cross one another**, that will secure sufficiently, however a little drop of seam sealant at the crossing will ensure this. Because you cannot back stitch with an overlock serger the following methods will finish the seam threads:

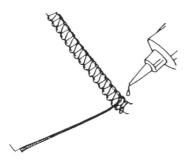

1. Use seam sealant, putting small dot (with toothpick) at beginning and end of seam. Let dry before trimming off excess, but if in a hurry you can use your hairdryer! If desired a knot can be tied first to ensure further the stability of this finish. Seam sealant dries hard and would irritate skin if placed at neck edge, etc. therefore methods 2 and 3 would be best.

2. The thread tails can be **threaded back into the seam** for about an inch, with a loop turner (my favourite), crochet hook or bodkin. Trim off excess.

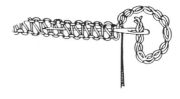

3. Secure the threads by **stitching over them** at beginning and end. At beginning take a couple stitches into fabric, stop, lift presser foot if desired, and fold 2″ (5cm) chain around to front, laying it next to seamline, being careful that chain does not extend to cutting blade for at least one inch (2.5cm). Continue stitching over chain. At the end, stitch off fabric for ½″ (1.3cm). Raise presser foot, gently pull threads off stitch finger (see page 79). Flip fabric over and to front of the machine, placing corner near needle, lower presser foot and stitch over previous stitching for about 1″ (2.5cm). Stitch off the fabric and trim off chain close to seam edge.

SEAM RIPPING

Stitches are easy to remove with overlocking machines, but once the fabric seam has been cut you can't add more! If you need a deeper seam allowance it is simply a case of stitching another row of serging which will trim off the unwanted amount. Should the stitch be improperly formed, use a seam ripper, as follows:

1. *Two-thread Overlock* — Slip seam ripper under looper stitches. Pull out cut threads.

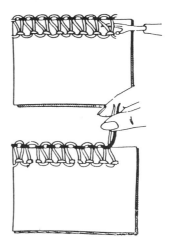

2. *Three-thread Overlock*— On top side of stitching, clip needle thread every few inches. At the seam edge, hold both the looper threads and pull them straight out. Then pull out remaining needle threads.

3. *Three/Four Thread Overlock* —
On top side of stitching, clip both needle threads every few inches. At the seam edge, hold both looper threads and pull straight out. Then pull out remaining needle threads.

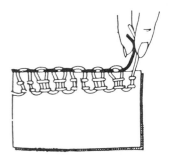

4. *Four-thread Overlock* — Working from underside, pull on the looper thread to remove the chain. Slip seam ripper under overedge stitch, then pull out cut threads.

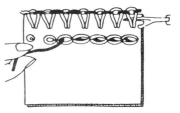

CONTINUOUS STITCHING

Because the chain of thread is a knitted type of stitch, it is not necessary to lift presser foot at the start of each seam. **Leave a chain of thread** between each piece if you need to secure stitches later, butting up next piece to front of presser foot. The feed dogs being considerably longer than a conventional machine, grab the cloth, evenly feeding it through the machine. However, if stitching a thick seam where the fabric would be pushed at the start, it is advisable to lift the foot and slip the seam up to the cutting blade to secure. **Do not pull fabric as this can break the needle.** This method is time-saving and easy to learn.

CORNERS

Inside Corners are covered in the Basic T-shirt chapter page 89. The same principles will apply to finishing corners without ribbing or trim. If you want a square or V-neck dress, top or babies bib, with exposed edges, this would be the technique used.

Outside Corners can be finished in two ways:

1 Stitch along one side of fabric and chain off the end. Then stitch the next side, crossing the stitching at the corner. Continue in like manner with remaining two edges. If using a tiny rolled edge, you can trim chains off at corners,

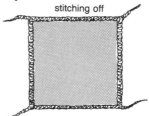

stitching off

using a dab of seam sealant. If using a regular overlock stitch you may want to thread chains back into seam.

2. Trim first and successive corners parallel to edge for about 1" (2.5cm) or a bit more, on seam allowance line. If stitching on outside edge with no seam allowance, this step is not necessary.

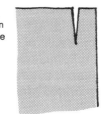

cut seam allowance

Stop when you reach the end of the fabric at corner. Lift presser foot. Pull needle thread slightly in front (if pulled too much you will have a thread loop at corner) and clear stitch fingers (see preceding page). If trimming a seam allowance, pull snipped seam allowance out of way, turn fabric carefully and place needle right at edge of previous stitching. It takes practice to judge this step! Lower the presser foot and continuing serging.

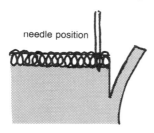

needle position

finished corner

COLLARS

Collars with facings are easy to apply with a serger.

1. Stitch outer edges of collar and turn right side out.

2. Stay stitch complete neck edge ½" (1.3cm) into seam allowance. Clip neck edge every inch (2.5cm) to stay stitching.

3. Pin collar to neck right sides together matching notches and markings.

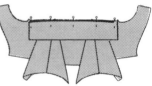

4. Fold front facings at fold lines and line up seam allowances on top of pinned collar. Fold back seam allowance on facing ends as shown. This is one spot where a machine basting stitch on a regular machine would be advisable.

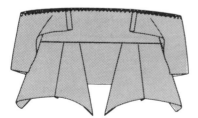

5. Serge stitch entire neck edge with narrow stitch.

6. Turn to right side and press.

CUFFS

Cuffs can be applied in a similar manner to collar. This speeds up the sewing tremendously.

Basic T-Shirt

CONVENTIONAL MACHINE METHOD

1. Cut out according to directions on page 36.

2. Stitch shoulder seams, right sides together using appropriate stitch, conventional machine page 47.

3. Stitch (pre-measured band - see page 51) banding or neck trim together to form a circle, using a straight stitch. Trim seam to ¼" (6mm) and press seam open. Fold band (with wrong sides together) double on lengthwise direction.

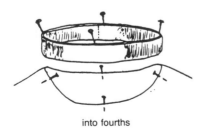

ends stitched

4. Divide the unfolded edge of neck band into fourths using pins as markers. Divide neck opening into fourths, (with wrong side of shirt facing out). Set neckband inside neck opening, (matching pins) placing ribbing seam at centre back, or on a side seam.

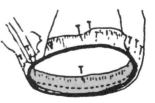

into fourths

RIBBING STITCHED

5. Stitch with strongest stitch available. If using a straight stitch go over seam several times, stretching as you stitch. Press seam toward shirt, over tailor's ham.

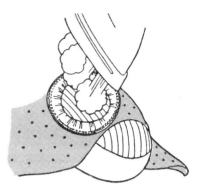

6. Match sleeve center with shoulder and pin. Sew sleeve in place while matching center-top sleeve to shoulder and underarm seams, stretching to fit armhole. This is referred to as the "shirt-sleeve" or flat method. Press seam toward sleeve.

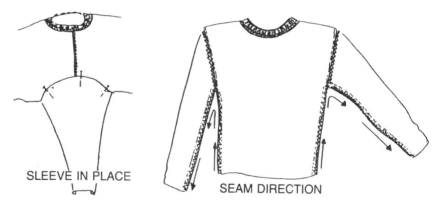

SLEEVE IN PLACE

SEAM DIRECTION

7. Sew side seams and sleeve together starting at bottom of garment body, continuing around to bottom of sleeve (cuff area). Press seam toward sleeve. Stitch a second row ¼" (6mm) away using a multiple or regular zig-zag. For T-shirt trim seam to ¼" (6mm). For a dress or jacket, trim underarm seam allowance between notches to ¼" (6mm).

8. Press seam allowances together on inside steaming fullness, pointing iron just ½" (1.3cm) into sleeve cap. Working on wrong side, put ham underneath and lightly steam, pushing seam allowances toward sleeve. No top pressing should be required.

9. Finish sleeve and bottom hem as desired. See page 108.

10. Ribbing may be applied to sleeve and bottom hem edges using same principle as neck application (see pages 51 and 52).

OVERLOCK SERGING MACHINE METHOD

"Flat method" construction is advisable when using an overlock machine. This will eliminate the need for finishing ends of seams as you sew over them when you cross the stitching lines. With regular sewing, it is customary to stitch a hem in a circular direction, which on a serger would mean overlapping your stitching to start and finish. **If you plan the order of construction you can eliminate many tricky sewing areas.**

A three or three/four thread machine gives good stretch. A four thread machine does not have enough stretch for ribbing and areas of stress. A complete shirt can be constructed without the use of your regular machine.

1. Stitch one shoulder seam.

2. Divide neck into fourths with pins, as well as pre-measured ribbing. See Ribbing chapter.

3. Clear stitch fingers (see page 80) to allow fabric and ribbing to slide under presser foot.

4. Apply ribbing to neckline using flat method, stretching ribbing in front of machine only, making it fit between pins. It is advisable to use ¼" (6mm) seam allowances as ribbing distorts when stretched and it is difficult to gauge the amount to be cut off. Ribbing has terrific stretch when stitched to a garment on the overlock serger. No popped stitches anymore! Remember: Don't forget to remove pins as you come to them!

5. Stitch other shoulder seam, continuing through band. Do not use seam sealant to finish serging seam at neckline. It could be irritating. Thread chain stitch back through with loop turner or needle.

6. Apply band to bottom of sleeves, or choose one of the hems from Chapter 20.

7. Stitch sleeves to garment using flat method, page 86.

8. Stitch side and sleeve seams continuing through band or hem.

9. Finish hem edge with hem of your choice, page 20.

SEWING ORDER

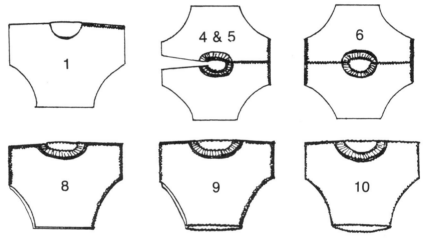

10. Stitch remaining side & sleeve seam through hem.

If desired, you can have **exposed seams** on your shirt. Use a perle cotton in both the upper and lower loopers for a more decorative appearance.

V-NECK OPENINGS WITH RIB OR SELF TRIM

Sewing a V-neck with a knit fabric is simplified in that you can leave the ribbing in one continuous piece, joining at one shoulder seam only.

1. Flat measure (walk around) the opening with a folded piece of ribbing, stretching slightly at back of neck and less on the side fronts.

2. Taking ¼" (6mm) seam, start sewing at one shoulder, ribbing on top of right side, stretching rib in front of machine the amount you measured, till you get to within 1" (2.5cm) of V.

3. Raise the presser foot so you may move the right hand side of V (or corner) till it is in straight line with stitching. You will now have a bubble of fabric at the point of V (or corner)....not to worry, this will vanish when stitching is completed. However, take minimal seam allowance at corner. If you are using a firm knit or a ⅝" (1.5cm) seam allowance, it may be necessary to clip into corner.

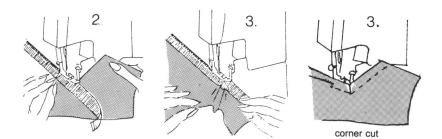

corner cut

4. After finishing stitching to other shoulder, stitch shoulder seams together. Thread stitching at neck edge back through serging, with loop turner.

5. Fold front of garment right sides together and straight stitch with conventional machine through banding, in line with centre fold.

6. Proceed to assemble garment with steps 5 through 7 in preceeding Overlock T-Shirt method.

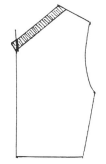

RIBBING V STITCHED

Sweater Knits

Sweater knits are very plentiful for the homesewer. You can duplicate very expensive jacquard sweaters, ribbed sweater dresses and metallic knits for one-half the price. Sweater knits do not ravel as you would think, but are easily cut out as any other knit. Overlock serging methods are great for putting it altogether and finishing.

Knit your own **sweater yardage** in a rectangular piece and then cut out with your pattern. This is much quicker! Knitting machines can whip out pieces like this in no time. If you purchase a patterned knit, hand-knit your own ribbing to match for the big foldover necklines and cuffs.

SWEATER SEAMS

Refer to Seam Finishes chapter for guidelines for your type of machine. Contrary to most thinking, it is not desirable to have excessively stretchy seams. Cut sweater knits with wider seam allowances as the seams do not stretch as much if sewn a distance from the edge. Stitching a short straight stitch with conventional machine on the seamline makes it easier to sew your multiple, reverse cycle or serged stitch beside. Your serger will trim off the excess or use scissors if using conventional stitches. In areas where extremely stretchy knits are used, the use of a 4-thread Overlock Serger would **stabilize the seams**.

Test Seam stitches with scraps of fabrics before using garment pieces. It is advisable to use one of the new basting tapes to hold seams together as pins can get lost in sweater knits. Generally a heavy fabric needs more pressure. Adjustment may be needed.

> KNIT TIP: *Avoid purchasing knits that are badly stretched out of shape. Unlike wovens they cannot be straightened!*

STABILIZING

Stay stitching is necessary with many of the loose knits to keep the curved edges from stretching. It is sometimes desirable to fuse an entire piece of sweater knit prior to sewing. This eliminates any irritation to the skin if a wooley

INTERFACED

texture, and also stabilizes the garment. If desired, just the shoulder, upper back or neck area could be interfaced. The fusible tricot knit type interfacings would be best as they give a soft hand which does not take away the supple look of the knit.

It is necessary to stabilize the shoulder seams with twill tape or by adding a crochet cotton strand to the seam. Serge over top.

cotton strand

DECORATIVE SEAMS

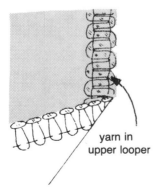

yarn in
upper looper

Refer to Lapped seams in Chapter 13. This gives a sporty look. Use lightweight sock yarn in both loopers or just the upper looper. This can finish the neckedge to tie in nicely with colour of sweater. The widest stitch gives a more effective finish. If desired an elastic thread can be placed under stitching to pull in a neckline or armhole edge.

SWEATER BANDING

This can be cut across the grain (with stretch) from fabric and sewn around the neck and fronts of a jacket or sweater. Fuse inter-facing only to area of band where buttonholes will be sewn before sewing band. Apply band with serger stitch or regular machine

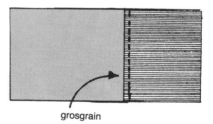

self rib applied

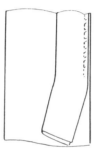

stitch with an overcast. You may top stitch with wide twin needle catching in seam allowance underneath.

For a straight front edge of a jacket sweater you may wish to use pre-shrunk or polyester grosgrain ribbon to finish. It is very easy to apply and acts as a perfect stabilizer for buttonholes.

grosgrain

1. Sew straight stitch down sweater front ⅜" (1cm) from edge.

2. Overlap wrong side of grosgrain to right side of sweater knit ⅜" (1cm).

3. Flat stitch ⅛" seam on grosgrain, through sweater knit.

4. Fold back grosgrain to wrong side of sweater. Buttons and buttonholes will hold it in place...no need to sew down.

5. Finish neck with self trim. See Chapter 11.

See Page 54, Sweater Makeovers.

Pressing

"Pressing as you sew" is the key to a **professional** looking garment. However, over-pressing creates a worn look. Even though knits are somewhat "unstructured", pressing will give them a finished look. Heavy pressing as used in tailoring techniques is not generally recommended. However, some of the same items used for pressing will make your sewing more enjoyable.

1. *Tailors Ham:* Oval style in shape to give those areas such as darts, curved areas, neck openings, the conture needed for that professional appearance.

2. *Seam Roll:* Long cylindrical roll primarily used in pressing seams so edges do not show through. Use in pressing narrow sleeve seams and pant legs.

3. *Point Presser:* Very helpful in pressing seams open in corners such as collars and tabs. A **Clapper** is often part of this unit (forming a base) which assists in retaining steam in seam to help flatten.

4. *Press Mitt:* This padded mitt slips into hard to reach areas or under the garment for a light steam press from right side in final touch up and finish. It can be slipped over end of sleeve board.

5. *Steam Iron:* The newer, shot-of-steam irons are excellent. The more holes the better. Steam is better for knits than a heavy damp press cloth as this could stretch fabric from resulting moisture and pressure.

6. *Press Cloths:* Lightweight, see-through press cloths are best. Cotton Batiste, and old diapers make excellent press cloths too! The woven rather than non-woven types are best. To avoid stretching, use steam but don't slide iron on fabric.

7. *Velvaboard:* Ideal for velours and napped fabrics as it has bristles on the pad which lifts fabric and thus avoids crushing while pressing.

8. *Sleeveboard:* Used for pressing sleeves and other hard to reach hems (e.g. cuffs). Can be used with press mitts, placed over board end.

> *Knit Tip:* Silicone finishes on Ironing Board covers do not allow the steam to penetrate into the garment. Sometimes the finish will come off leaving gold or silver specks on your garment. Cotton makes the best cover.

DART PRESSING

Darts should be sewn with regular stitch to within ½" (1.3cm) of end. Change at that point to a tiny stitch running off end of dart and letting the threads twist. Cut the ends leaving a ½"(1.3cm) tail. Press dart (from wrong side), folded edge flat in the same position as stitched. This will help to smooth stitching and flatten fold.

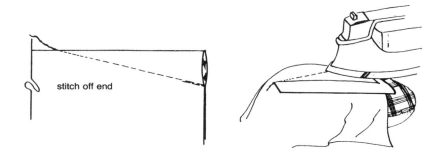

stitch off end

Place garment and dart over a tailor's ham. Place dart end at ham end and press dart down if horizontal or to centre for vertical darts. Placing a piece of brown paper under dart will eliminate a line showing through. Turn to right side and top press, using a press cloth. If dart edge still shows through return to the underside and press on garment side, steaming out line.

Knit Tip: Do not allow garment to "hang" over the ironing board while pressing, as this will stretch the garment and give a baggy look.

Elastic Applications

Chlorine treated, Ban-roll and the new transparent elastics give the most satisfactory long-term results.

New Transparent Elastic comes only in narrow widths up to ⅝″(12mm) but has some very unique features.

- Sewing on it does not weaken elasticity. It retains perfect memory and wearability.

- Excellent for aerobic and swimwear as chlorine does not seem to affect durability.

- Overlock elastic serging foot makes a perfect elasticator for the ⅜″ (10mm) or ¼″ (6mm) widths. See Page 68. Serger will cut off elastic easily if you wish.

- Doesn't pinch or feel tight when wearing which makes it perfect for babies and children's clothing as well as the lightweight softness for lingerie.

- Sheer weight fabrics such as georgette or 15 denier tricot are less bulky with this elastic. The transparency will yellow slightly over a period of time so you may consider this if putting it in a pure white sheer fabric.

As for most leg or neck openings, use two-thirds of opening for elastic measurement. Measure stretch around opening to see how it will look and compare the two-thirds ratio. This would apply to waist also, although skirts and slacks are better with a ¾″(2cm) or 1″ (2.5cm) width for stability, thus chlorine treated elastic is best if you wish an enclosed stitched finish.

ENCLOSED ELASTIC

Elasticized edges perfectly suit the comfortable, stretchable nature of knits. For a snug, flexible edge on closely fitted knit garments, leg openings, swim suits, waistband edges on skirts or slacks, use this method for elastic application for a neat, firm finish. Ensure the elastic used is durable as this edge is difficult to remove. Chlorine treated elastic stands up well and may be used on any garment, not just swim suits. As firmer elastics cannot be penetrated, use chlorine, transparent type or lingerie elastic for zig-zag application. If using lingerie elastic take 4 to 6 inches (10 to 15.3cm) less or two-thirds of opening measurement for easy calculation. Stitching two rows tends to stretch out elastic so it is very important to **cut down** on your usual elastic measurement.

1. Overlap elastic ends and stitch back and forth using a zig-zag stitch. A multiple zig-zag is best.

2. Divide the elastic circle and garment edge in fourths, using pins as markers.

3. Pin elastic to garment outside, having picot edge facing down toward garment if using lingerie elastic, and straight edge at top, matching pin markers.

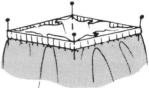

4. Stretch both elastic and garment, stitching the elastic in place, close to picot or bottom edge. Use a tiny regular zig-zag or a multiple zig-zag. Should any of the raw edge protrude beyond elastic, trim away. **Serger method:** Stitch along top edge, stretching elastic in front of presser foot only, using longest stitch length. Can use elastic foot, see page 68. Machine trims off any excess seam allowance as you are sewing. With elastic and regular presser foot, it takes practice to gauge the distance between the elastic and cutting blade. Turn blade out of way till you can master this. Transparent elastic solves this problem as sergers can cut and sew this very easily.

5. Fold elastic to inside and stitch again (with conventional machine) close to straight edge. This completely encloses elastic placing raw edge to inside of garment. The use of a twin needle on top with your regular thread and "Wooley Nylon"™ in the bobbin gives the nicest finish as well as maximum elasticity for this step. See page 115.

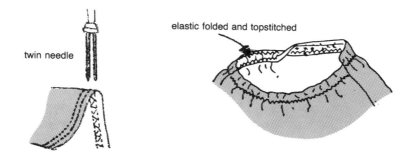

twin needle

elastic folded and topstitched

CASING METHOD

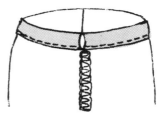

This method is best for garments constructed with a straight sewing machine. Sew all seams on garment, side seams, centre front or sleeve seams as applicable.

1. Fold garment top edge over the width of elastic plus seam allowance.

2. Garment edge may be finished with zig-zag stitch or a row of straight stitches (as available).

3. Sew with a straight stitch (small zig-zag) close to waist raw edge, leaving a small opening near a seam allowance.

4. Insert elastic through opening and pull ends out. Overlap ends and stitch together (zig-zag or a multiple stitch). No-roll or Ban-roll elastics are best for waist, with this method.

5. Tuck elastic up in place and stitch across small area left open for elastic insertion.

SERGER CASING METHOD — for Waist

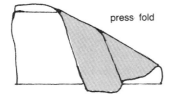

press fold

I. Fold over garment top edge width of elastic plus seam allowance, then take folded waistband and bring it back to right side of garment. Press.

2. Place elastic inside band section, pinning as necessary, allowing seam allowance to extend beyond top of garment.

3. Stitch on serger along top of fold from wrong side of garment, being careful not to catch elastic into stitching. Stop stitching about 4" (10.2cm) before starting point.

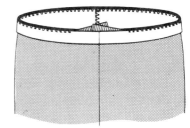

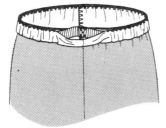

4. Try on garment and pull elastic to fit. Overlap elastic ends ½" (1.3cm) and stitch with zig-zag stitch (regular machine). Tuck inside band.

5. Finish serging the opening.

You can apply a **separate waistband** in a similar manner, however, if using an elasticized waistband, it is advisable to cut waistband onto the garment, eliminating extra pieces.

SHIRRED CASING

This finish gives a soft gathered look for waists or cuff finishing. Use the regular casing method, but stitch rows of straight stitching around band. Thread elastic through tunnels. Overlap and stitch together. Close opening on casing by hand stitching. Stitch-in-the-ditch at side seams through all layers to keep elastic from twisting. See page 52.

LINGERIE

We refer you to our **Silks 'N Satins** book Chapter I8, which has all the techniques needed to create gorgeous lingerie. Although it is geared for "woven" fabrics, nylon tricot works just as well. Even the Teddy is great made in a silk knit, or tricot. The only part which would not be necessary is bias cut garments as knits have stretch already.

If you do not have a serger, a narrow zig-zag seam (page 48) works perfectly. Tricot does not stretch on the vertical, only on the crosswise grain so you may need to keep edges "taut" while sewing.

In the Fashion Ideas chapter, page 123, we give ideas for mock French hand sewing done on the serger with laces and trims.

> *Knit Tip:* **Which hem should I use?** Personal rule of thumb is to use a machine hem if garment is to be washed. If it will be drycleaned, a hand sewn hem is more effective and elegant in appearance.

Zippers

EXPOSED APPLICATION

This application is used when there is **no center back seam.** This is suitable for small neck openings, with use of stripes, and high turtle neck styles.

1. Place a piece of "Scotch Magic tape"™ alongside the center back line, the length of zipper plus top seam allowance or turtle neck depth. The metal piece at zipper bottom will be exposed.

TAPE PLACEMENT

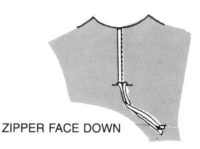

ZIPPER FACE DOWN

2. With zipper top facing garment bottom, place right side of zipper on right side of fabric.

3. Attach zipper foot to machine. Using very tiny stitches, sew just the width of zipper metal end.

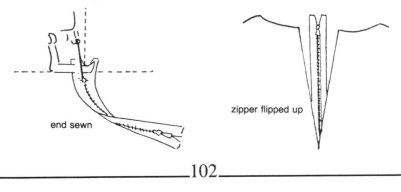

end sewn

zipper flipped up

4. Cut down center back, close to tape edge, to the metal tab already sewn in position. Remove tape from right side and turn zipper up and into position on your garment.

5. Taking just ⅛" **(3mm)** seam allowance, tapering to nothing at bottom end, stitch close to teeth using a zipper foot. Pull bottom corner to ensure no tuck is made. Use "magic transparent" or wash-a-way "Wonder tape" to hold in place, thus eliminating basting. Carefully match stripes (if applicable). Any stitched pieces of tape will come off in first washing.

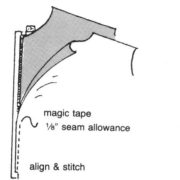

magic tape
⅛" seam allowance

align & stitch

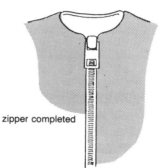

zipper completed

REGULAR LAPPED APPLICATION

1. Must have minimum ⅝" (1.5cm) seam allowance (¾" (2cm) is better). Measure and mark exact length of placket opening using zipper (with pull tab up), plus seam allowance. Mark this length on garment seam. Stitch seam closed with regular stitching, back tack, then change to a long basting stitch for zipper placket.

2. Press open seam and remove basting stitches in placket area by clipping bottom stitch and pulling from the top.

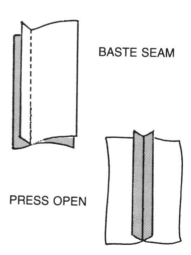

BASTE SEAM

PRESS OPEN

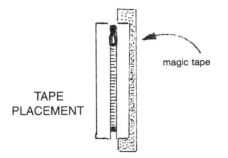

magic tape

TAPE
PLACEMENT

3. Position a piece of transparent tape to cloth edge on to cloth edge on right-hand side of zipper back. Half of tape edge extends beyond zipper tape.

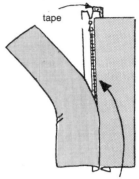

tape

fold pressed to zippper tape

4. Working from right side, place folded edge of garment opening close to zipper teeth, pressing the tape to back of seam allowance. The tape holds zipper in position acting as basting.

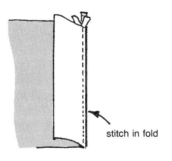

stitch in fold

5. Using zipper foot, turn up seam allowance and sew in fold from right side (pressed crease). To start sewing, pull zipper tab slightly down, leaving needle in fabric, while you pull it up when you reach the tab. **There are no stitches visible on right side with this in-the-fold sewing method.**

If desired, you may sew on right side of fabric close to zipper teeth rather than by above method. Sewing from behind is by far the nicest method for couture garments.

6. Place the folded edges together, on right side overlapping slightly to hide zipper. Tape the edges together. Topstitch ¼" (6mm) to ⅜" (1cm) over from folded edge, through all thicknesses (use zipper foot) starting from the bottom. When you reach tab, release it; pull tab down and carefully finish stitching to top. **Presto!** A completed zipper **without** basting!

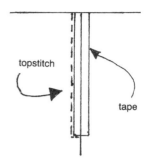

PRICKSTITCH

7. Hand topstitching on final step gives your garment a couturier look. Use a tiny, prick stitch. Insert needle through all layers to right side. Reinsert a few threads behind and bring up approximately ¼" **(3mm)** ahead of first stitch. To give added strength, you may sew a row of machine stitching behind, joining seam allowance and zipper tape together.

Centred application is desirable for centre back on garments. See Silks 'N Satins Book, Zippers.

PATTERN PIECES MIXED UP? *Place a piece of "Scotch magic tape" on the wrong side of fabric. You can label each piece as this tape has a dull finish which can be written on.*

Machine Buttonholes

BUTTONHOLE PLACEMENT

Horizontal buttonholes should begin ⅛″ (3mm) over centre front line toward garment edge. Button shank will then sit in centre position.

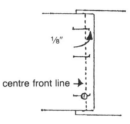

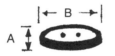

$A + B + ⅛″(3mm) =$ Length
BUTTONHOLE LENGTH

Measure button diameter plus thickness and add ⅛″ (3mm) to measurement.

Ensure facing area is interfaced to give stability. For horizontal buttonholes place non-stretch direction of interfacing with the same direction as buttonhole length. This eliminates the possibility of stretching buttonhole. For sweatery knits a ¾″ (2cm) piece of "transparent tape" on top of the garment will give the needed stability while sewing. Mark guidelines for sewing buttonhole on "tape". Stitch and Tear rip-away type backing can be used. It is possible to stitch perfect button-holes in the lightest of fabrics with this type of backing. Built-in

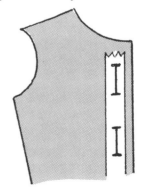

MARK HOLES ON TAPE

buttonholers are much more satisfactory than the attachment styles. Sew your buttonhole through the tape and garment fabric. Carefully tear tape from garment. Slit the buttonhole down the centre. Should you cut out a thread, return to machine and zig-zag slightly, or use one of clear seam sealants available. Many of the new computerized machines will sew continuous buttonholes the same size after you have programmed in the first one!

CORDED MACHINE BUTTONHOLES

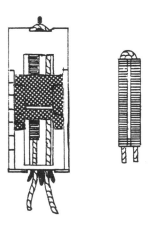

If your machine has a special buttonhole foot with a little hook on the back, you may loop a piece of buttonhole twist or fine cord around this and proceed to sew as usual. After the buttonhole is sewn, pull the cord, taking out any ripple or slack in buttonhole. Snip cords, and flatten buttonhole. Pulled cords will recede under stitching after they are snipped. This extra cord will keep buttonhole from stretching aside from giving it a nice rounded effect.

Knit Tip: If sewing buttonholes onto ribbing front of jacket or top, ensure that you place firm non-stretch interfacing into the area for the buttonholes. The ribbing causes buttonholes to be stretched out or "fish-mouthed"!

BOUND BUTTONHOLES

These are very easy and attractive for the more tailored double knit wool suits and dresses. A very easy method is found in the SILKS 'N SATINS book, page 81.

Hem Finishes

Allowing a garment to hang a day or so before hemming is advisable for dresses and jumpsuits. Pin hem in place before hanging as weight of hem can cause hemline to sink. You may need to re-pin to even the hem. Heavier knits, such as velours, stretch terry, sweater knits, etc. are especially susceptible. Hems for sportswear garments (e.g. t-shirts) are best done by machine. Several quick types are available. **Do not put seam binding on or turn edge under** on these garments.

INVISIBLE HEM

Fold up hem and fold back on itself allowing ¼" (6mm) or more to extend up from hemside. Use a zig-zag catching every second or third stitch on garment fold. If you have a built in blind hemmer, use that along with the special foot which has a guide for the fold of fabric.

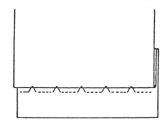

serged blind hem

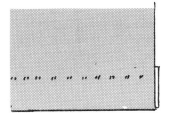

A serged blind hem can be done by folding same as above, being careful to just barely catch fold with stitches (loosen tensions). The longest stitch length would be best. This works well with knits. Some overlock machines have a special blind hem foot.

FLATLOCKED HEM

See page 77, for details on how to flatlock. Either side of the flatlock stitch can be used for the right side. The stitches are quite noticeable if you use the "ladder" on the right side. The looped stitch finish is quite sporty looking. Fold hem up and then back on itself. Stitch close to the folded edge of the fabric.

WELT HEM

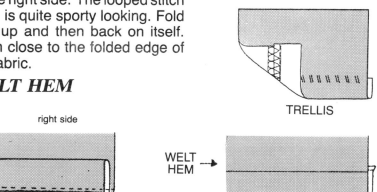

LOOP FLAT LOCK

TRELLIS

right side

WELT → HEM

Presents the illusion of extra fabric piece. On wrong side, turn up width of required hem and fold back an identical width on right side. Stitch along ⅛" (3mm) from raw edge through garment fold underneath. Then, press down hem. This can also be achieved by using a serger stitch along folded edge.

CUFF HEM

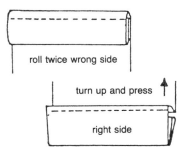

roll twice wrong side

turn up and press ↑

right side

Turn up width of hem twice and press, stitch ¼" (6mm) up from the bottom on fold with hem on machine bed. Press down hem. This hem needs ½" (1.3cm) extra allowance and is especially nice on short sleeves and plain fabrics.

TOPSTITCHED HEM

This quick method looks best on your casual outfits which have other topstitched details. Can be very narrow; just topstitch close to hem fold, then trim hem allowance close to stitching. As a design feature, vary the technique by using two or more rows of top stitching and a deeper hem.

ROLLED AND UNROLLED HEMS

These can be used with the rolled hemmer foot with conventional sewing machines. However, with most knits it tends to stretch the fabric. The rolled hems produced with overlock sergers are perfect for lighter weight knits. Ruffled hems give a soft finish and are best on lightweight jerseys sewn on the crossgrain or bias. See page 74.

BLIND CATCH STITCH HEM

This hand-stitched hem is best for dressier knits and wool doubleknits, etc. You may wish to finish hem edge by using one of the fancy machine stitches, such as a step or regular zig-zag, or an over-edge serging stitch. Turn up a hem width and then fold back ¼" (6mm) hem edge toward yourself on wrong side. Work from

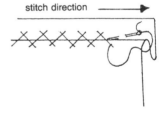

stitch direction

left to right with needle pointing left. Make a catch stitch (resembles cross stitch) underneath this area. **Important!** Keep this stitch loose and pick up **only** one thread on the garment side. To keep stitches from showing or breaking as you move, do not pull threads tightly as hem needs to have some built-in "give".

Use a double catch stitch hem, if required for a heavier fabric, with one row 1" (2.5cm) from bottom and a second row ¼"(6mm) down from hem top. Leaving the ¼" (6mm) allows the option of running an iron between hem and garment which eliminates a ridge showing.

Action Wear

BODY SUITS

Action wear terminology varies in North America. Body suits are commonly referred to as leotards in the U.S., while in Canada leotards are tights. For our purposes, we will use the terms Bodysuits and Tights, to avoid confusion. Availability of many new, exciting fabrics and bodysuit patterns has revitalized this whole area. The "fitness fever" is involving the whole family. Like the quote, "look the part — feel the part", an attractive, personalized bodysuit enhances the enjoyment and enthusiasm for exercise. We include a unique sampling of 12 bodysuit styles which may easily be adapted to your basic bodysuit pattern. (see page 119)

FABRICS

Two-Way Stretch fabrics must be used to give comfort and stretch-ability required for movement. Many blends are available; nylon-lycra, poly-cotton lycra and polyester lycra or spandex styles. Swimwear fabrics are suitable but most enthusiasts prefer cotton blends which "breathe". Combination of dots, stripes and many vivid colours create an exciting fashion effect.

PATTERN STYLES

There are not a great many commercial patterns on the market but we feature all current ones in our Seminars. Personal comfort will be your guide in choice of styles; cap sleeve, sleeveless, long sleeve, two-piece or bathing suit style with thin straps (worn bra-less so keep in mind if extra support is needed). Leg cuts also vary. A high leg style will require use of tights to avoid showing a panty line.

SIZING

It is not feasible to present a rigid set of sizing instructions due to the great variance in the amount of stretch for each fabric. There are, however, some applicable guidelines (refer to pages 8 and 12) or to the stretch gauge on pattern envelope. Ensure your fabric has the equivalent amount of stretch. Some patterns have two-way stretch gauges. **For bodysuits, the greatest stretch will go around your body. For tights, the stretch should be the greatest running vertically.** The majority of bodysuit patterns feature multiple sizing. This makes adjustments easy if you are different sizes on top and bottom. **A comparative measurement of your body with pattern measurements cannot be done for this type of garment.** Patterns are designed, incorporating the stretch factor and thus, will be slightly shorter in length (normally 1″ in total length). The waist widths also vary. To illustrate; pull your fabric across grain, 4 inches down from a folded edge and observe the length pulling up.

FITTING

Crotch length: Tie a string around waist. From this point measure from center front, through crotch up to center back. It should measure ½″ to 1″ less than your pattern-flat measured. If longer, you may shorten later. If shorter, always cut on appropriate line and reduce. You add one-half amount required on each piece, front and back to increase. As a precaution, you may add ½″ extra to front and back leg and crotch seam allow-ance when cutting. Remove during fitting as required. Some patterns have crotch length mea-surements listed separately so match up yours to determine correct size. This eliminates pattern flat measuring.

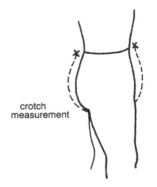

crotch measurement

Back Length: Compare your own measurements to those on chart on pattern envelope back. If your actual measurement taken from top of backbone to waist varies make the necessary changes before laying out and cutting.

Waist Measurement: In as much as you cannot achieve an accurate true reading from measuring pattern verses your own, I have found 3 inches less (approximately) works well with the majority of two-way stretch fabrics (these have tremendous give on the crossgrain).

Tracing Off Pattern: Trace whole front and back of pattern (if these pieces are shown on fold) using tracing cloth of your choice. If there are center front and back seams, these will be in two pieces and have some shaping. If you plan to customize by cutting different lines (using several colours, stripes, dots, etc.) the full front is easier to use for lines.

Sample Suit: We personally recommend purchase of an inexpensive remnant for a trial body suit. From this basic fit you can adjust your sizing as necessary to accommodate stretch variations for successive garments. If you are a fairly accurate size and fit according to pattern measurements, the knit will cover most minor problems. You are now ready to plunge in with a more expensive fabric and personalized styling.

STITCHES

Reverse Cycle Stitches: are the most desirable when using a conventional sewing machine, giving the most stretch. Refer to page 48 for edge overcast or overlock stretch stitches. As reverse stitches give sufficient elasticity, it is not necessary to stretch fabric while sewing.

Zig-Zag: Sew seams with very narrow zig-zag and medium stitch length, stretching fabric slightly as you sew. Overcast seam allowances together with a larger zig-zag stitch.

Straight Stitching: is not recommended for this type of fabric as seams pop under stress. If you must use this stitch, stretch seam considerably as you sew it, doing your second row near seam allowance edge. One quarter (¼″) inch seam allowances are customary.

Overlock Machines: A three thread stitch has the most elasticity. These machines give the most elastic stitch possible for two-way stretch fabrics. A three/four thread machine will also be stretchy but not quite as much as the three thread. The speed and finish makes sewing these garments a breeze! See pages 58 & 59 for information.

Construct bodysuit as shown in pattern. Prior to finishing neck and leg areas try on and make any adjustments before installation of elastics.

ELASTIC APPLICATIONS

See page 97. Until you have determined your exact fit, we personally prefer a casing application which makes for easy adjustment of length. Use a tiny zig-zag, stretching as you sew, for your top-stitching elasticity. Use a **chlorine treated**elastic for durability and long wear, or the new **"transparent"**thin elastic which is less bulky and perfect for swim and action wear. See page 97, elastics.

Topstitching — The newest method for **finishing outer edges** of swimsuits and bodysuits is as follows:

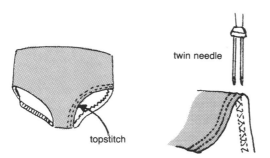

twin needle

topstitch

1. Follow basic elastic measurements and application page 98.

2. Serge or stretch stitch elastic to wrong side of edge, stitching with elastic side up, stretching to fit fabric.

3. Turn both fabric and elastic to wrong side.

4. With twin needle (not too wide) threaded with regular polyester thread and "wooley nylon" on bobbin, stitch from right side. The twin needle stitching forms a type of zig-zag on the underside, coupled with the stretchiness of the "wooley nylon" to give an extremely elasticized stitch.

TIGHTS

The majority of the stretch should run vertically, down the leg. The pattern you choose should be for a two-way stretch fabric which allows for this. Compare the stretch gauge on the pattern with your fabric, as they should fit as their name, "tight".

Bathing suit prints, stripes, plains are all suitable in the nylon/lycra type, or you can also use the poly/cotton/lycra blend which is lighter weight and will breathe. For joggers, because of the nylon content, the heat is retained inside, thus keeping the muscles warm. Recently I saw a male mountain climber in the Rockies wearing 2" (5cm) hot pink and black striped tights in nylon/lycra. He was delayed in his climb and we were able to spot him for miles without binoculars! Apparently the comfort is tremendous as well as the fact that the fabric doesn't seem to snag when it is so close to the body. Cutting fabric on bias gives even more elasticity.

The mid-calf length is popular at this writing, worn with midriff tops. Whatever the style, your **overlock serger** can simplify the process for construction.

- If in doubt on the sizing, make a bit longer. You can take up at waist, prior to putting elastic in place, or delete at ankle or stirrup pieces.

- Finish bottom edges with serger, either straight across or stirrup type.

- Usually patterns for tights have no side seam. Sew inner leg seams.

- Place one leg inside the other, right sides together and sew the crotch seam.

- Measure elastic approximately 1½" (3.7cm) less than waist measurement. Overlap ½" (1.2cm) to form circle and stitch with conventional machine.

- Try on tights at this stage, placing elastic at top of waist. Pull up any excess to make for a good fit. Mark with invisible pen. Trim off excess beyond top of elastic or trim when stitching with serger.

- Follow directions for elastic application page 97.

- Lastly fit and sew the stirrup if you have one, or turn under regular straight leg and finish with twin-needle method for topstitching in this chapter.

Crotch Lining: If desired, a piece of cotton stretch knit may be cut and placed inside crotch area to give added protection. Use your pattern pieces to cut out shape and if seam is made, put it wrong side to wrong side when placing in suit. High leg styles should have crotch lining in event you decide not to wear tights. Crotch linings may also be placed in tights.

Padded Bias Armhole Trim: "**Couture Comfort Finish**"! Cut strip of bias 2 inches (5cm) less than armhole measurement and 2 inches (5cm) in width. Stitch ends together to form a circle. Cut ½ inch (5cm) wide strip of polyester fibre fill approximately 1 inch (2.5cm) thick. Lay fill in the center of bias strip, pushing to round in center. Fold bias strip over and stitch (2 long edges on right side) with long basting stitch ⅛ inch (3mm) in from edge. Divide armhole and bias in half. Place trim on right side of suit matching halves and stitch in a ¼" (6mm) seam. If you have a ⅝" (1.5cm) seam allowance, trim back to a ¼" (.5cm) prior to stitching in place, so that both edges can be aligned together. If you are using a serger, then serge close to the edge, trimming slightly. See suit No. 2 on page 119.

Headband: A padded or plain headband can be created using similar method to padded bias techniques.

Leg Warmers: Matching or contrasting leg warmers are easily made using self fabric or sweater knits. Take measurements off a pair that you have, or fit fabric around leg pinning for the look you wish. Generally a piece of elastic sewn in a casing at the top and bottom will keep the warmer from sliding down the leg.

PERSONALIZING TO SUIT YOU

Refer to page 119 for sample ideas for designs created by cutting your patterns. Save your scraps and use as combinations (print and colour ways). When cutting diagonally, fold on the true bias, adding seam allowances to both sides. If stripes are on bias or vertical you will have more vertical stretch and, therefore, a decrease in body length may be required. Horizontal, vertical or bias cuts may be incorporated ... **just remember to cut seam allowances on edges as you cut**. Stitch them back together and **you have created your own personalized design in a bodysuit!**

> *Knit Tip:* If you have pinned garment together for sewing, ensure pins are removed prior to stitching over them or this will dull your needle, causing "runs" in fabric.

Personalizing to suit you

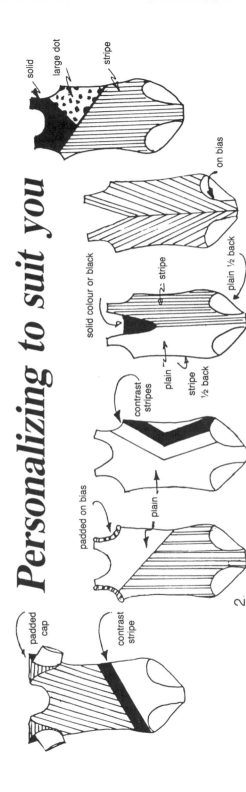

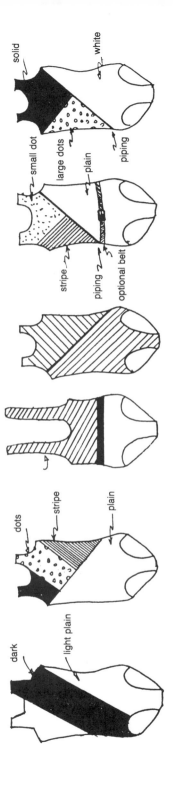

2.

Fashion Ideas

TUBE COLLAR

This collar can be worn neatly folded over giving a "turtle neck" look or folded softly (almost a single thickness) giving a "cowl" effect by rolling top and bottom edges under.

1. Cut a piece of fabric 24″ (61cm) by 12″ to 18″ (30.5 to 45.7cm) deep either crosswise or lengthwise. This can be made larger if a draping effect is desired so experiment and decide which suits you best.

2. Stitch shorter edges right sides together with a straight stitch, pulling seam slightly as you sew. Stitch and press open.

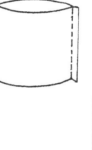

3. Fold to wrong side ¼″ (6mm) to ⅜″ (8mm) a hem on both ends of tube. Machine stitch close to unfinished edge and turn right side out.

This finished collar is pulled **over** the head and lays loosely on top of garment, allowing a fuller look or a plain neck depending on desired mood. See front cover graphic for suggested finished look and effect.

DECORATIVE FANCY TOPS

Machine Applique

APPLIQUE

Refer to Silks 'N Satins page l28, Machine applique. Many of the most attractive and expensive knit tops (often poly/cotton interlock) have strips of varying colours appliqued onto the side front. Choose scraps of fabric for this technique and woven fusible interfacing on the back. It is easier to fuse a piece of fabric and then cut out design. Appliques may be padded for more effect. Use stitch and tear behind your stitching and you will have no problems with the garment stretching out.

Use a small piece of "Scotch magic tape" to secure the ends of thread on spools. Keeps your sewing drawer tidy and organized.

Rhinestone applicator machines are available to purchase, or you can sometimes rent the use of one from a fabric store specializing in this type of item. There are several sizes that work for each machine and sew-on larger types can also be purchased.

RHINESTONES

The shoulders are perfect for that special evening, or a spray to one side. Applique a design and then highlite a certain area with rhinestones. You will need to stabilize the wrong side with woven fusible interfacing to ensure that the rhinestones don't sink through the knit or woven fabric. Amazingly, if you turn your shirt or top inside out for washing the rhinestones stand up very well.

OVERLOCK SERGER IDEAS

Pintucking

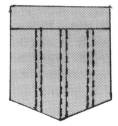

Pintucking is easiest done prior to cutting out the garment piece. Using the presser foot width as a a guide between the rows of tucking makes this much simpler than pressing folds. A narrow stitch is most attractive, as well as closing the stitch up to give a satin look.

Using metallic, rayon or shiney thread gives the tucks a decorative look. Use this in the upper looper and regular machine thread in the needle. Serge along the fold line being careful not to trim fold. If you can turn knife up out of way it would be advisable.

MOCK FRENCH HAND SEWING

Use different types of lace (insertion type best) and rows of rolled edge pintucks to create this old-fashioned look. Use it for yokes on nighties, blouses, children's clothing and dresses.

1. Plan for ¼" (6mm) seam allowance on fabric edges.

2. Set machine for narrow rolled hem close stitch length.

3. Place strip of fabric and lace wrong sides together; lace back from fabric edge ¼" (6mm)

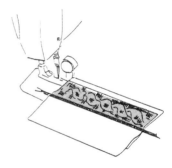

4. Place under presser foot with stitching catching lace on very edge and fabric seam allowance being trimmed away.

5. Turn panel around and place second piece of fabric on opposite side of lace, repeating step 4.

6. Fold fabric under to wrong side, the width of presser foot as a guide.

7. Let presser foot rest along previous line of rolled hemming and carefully stitch along fold.

8. Repeat as many rows of hemming (pintucking) as desired. Intersperse further rows of lace if desired.

Yardage lace can be made into beautiful trims by finishing the edges with this same rolled edge finish. A slip lace can be applied with this method. Put wrong sides together so edge will be on top or if using a two thread machine a small flat lock seam could be used. The latter does not give as finished a look.

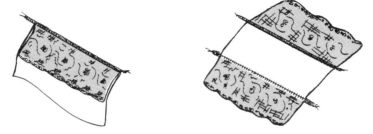

SERGER LACE APPLICATIONS

SHOULDER PAD CAMISOLE

In order to eliminate the need for putting shoulder pads in each garment, a shoulder pad camisole or teddy would simplify the work. Stretch lace in white, pastels and black are available, giving less bulk than most undergarments. The pattern companies are making patterns available for this item.

When cutting out your patterns use weights instead of pins to hold pattern pieces. Many European workrooms employ this method which can eliminate pinning delicate fabrics and simplify your layouts.

INDEX

AVAILABLE FROM TEX-MAR SEMINARS AND PUBLICATIONS

PUBLICATIONS

1. **"COUTURE ACTION KNITS", THE GUIDEBOOK TO SEWING WITH KNIT KNOW HOW"** , including Overlock Serging techniques, by **HAZEL BOYD HOOEY**

2. **"SILKS 'N SATINS — TWENTY-FOUR HOUR ELEGANCE", THE SEWING GUIDEBOOK TO FASHIONS IN SILK,** by **HAZEL BOYD HOOEY**

SEMINARS (Lecture, Slide and Fashion Show presentations)

1. **"COUTURE ACTION KNITS"**

2. **"SILKS 'N SATINS — TWENTY-FOUR HOUR ELEGANCE"**

For information on hosting a Tex-Mar seminar, to order publications, **OR TO PASS ON A COMMENT** contact:

**TEX-MAR SEMINARS AND PUBLICATIONS
#57 — 10220 DUNOON DRIVE
RICHMOND, BRITISH COLUMBIA
V7A 1V6**